Canadian Baseball
Hall of Fame

DIAMONDS
IN THE ROUGH

DIAMONDS IN THE ROUGH

by Ken Rappoport

tempo books

GROSSET & DUNLAP
A Filmways Company
Publishers • New York

To my own Triple-A Minors:

Felicia, Sharon, and Larry

Photographs (except where otherwise noted) by Ken Rappoport

Diamonds in the Rough

Copyright © 1979 by Ken Rappoport
All Rights Reserved
ISBN: 0-448-17343-3
A Tempo Books Original
Tempo Books is registered in the U.S. Patent Office
Published simultaneously in Canada
Printed in the United States of America

Contents

A selection of photographs begins opposite page 118.

Prologue

There was a time when it seemed that minor league baseball was dying.

Before, there had been nineteen solid leagues, flush with health, and the structure was steel-like. And then there was one, with a seemingly bleak future in store.

This was 1918.

But, as history shows, baseball has a wonderful ability to bounce back off the ground and dust itself off. In a few years, the minors took a sharp upswing in fortune. Postwar America boomed and so did the national pastime at the grass-roots level. By the late 1920s, there were some thirty leagues in full swing in the minors and blue skies ahead.

There is a feeling of déjà vu in this slice of sports history. Two decades later, the minor leagues once again were flourishing with intensity and soon thereafter went into a similar depression and had to be similarly revived again.

In 1949—perhaps the high point in minor league history—baseball was king with fifty-nine leagues,

448 teams, and untold thousands of players in the so-called bushes. But just ten years later, minor league baseball was on its back. Diminished to twenty-one leagues and less than half the players, the minors were knocked down again. But *not* knocked out, as subsequent history reveals.

Recognized as a necessity, the minors were fortified by major league teams and kept afloat through the 1960s. And by the 1970s, a leveling-off process had taken place. There were mild fluctuations, to be sure, with occasional league and team changes, but the base was strong enough to hold the structure—albeit a smaller structure. By 1978, there were only eighteen leagues and 158 teams left, but most of them were solidly entrenched.

In both low-water periods of the minor leagues, the condition of the country more than the condition of the sport played a major role in the dramatic changes. The National Association of Professional Baseball Leagues, the ruling body of the minors, had been rocking along steadily and serenely for several years before the crisis period of World War I. Only one league, the International, survived 1918.

The 1920s began a new era in the minors and the prosperous times were pushed along by the firm hand of Judge Kenesaw Mountain Landis, the exalted high commissioner of baseball. Landis's office solidified relations between the majors and minors with a new agreement, which has governed organized baseball with few alterations ever since.

The minors began to make noises again in the Roaring Twenties, shrugged off the Great Depression of the thirties, and coasted into the forties in explosive fashion. Starting with the Triple-A level, there were six degrees of baseball proficiency down to Class D ball. And most everybody was making money, especially the high minors where Triple-A teams were drawing upward of a half-million people a year. At one International League game, the 1941 opener of Rochester at Jersey City, 56,391 tickets were sold.

So it was with some degree of culture shock that business began to fall off in the fifties, a lush post-war period when theoretically it should have gotten better. What happened? Essentially, people turned from spectators to do-it-yourself sportsmen. With more money to burn, Americans took up golf, escaped in boats, went camping, and hit the open road looking for other entertainments than minor league baseball. Combined with the televised games of major league teams, which were now reaching a bigger market, the attraction of minor league ball was not so great. By 1959, more than half the leagues had been wiped out by public apathy.

Something had to be done, the major leagues knew, and therefore started pouring big money into minor league affiliations. This subsidization took place mainly in the area of salaries, the biggest single expense of any minor league team. The victim started showing a bit of color and after awhile, was up on its feet again.

The 1970s have been filled with intrigue and new melodrama. It seems that one major league figure or another is always trying to sabotage the minor league structure. There have been individual efforts by some to make further cutbacks in the system—

eliminate one of the three existing levels, for instance. (When the resolution to eliminate the Double-A level was recently brought up at a meeting of the Association, by the way, it was soundly defeated.) There have been proposals as well to wipe out the minor leagues altogether, one revolutionary concept embracing a baseball complex in Florida where players would be nurtured in virtual laboratory-type conditions.

But clear-thinking people are up in arms against this.

"Players have to develop under actual playing conditions," says Pat McKernan, the president of the Eastern League. "It's stupid to think otherwise. It doesn't make sense. What good does it do to develop warm-weather ballplayers and then bring them into the climate in which we play in the Eastern League? The Eastern League has to be in existence as long as there are teams in Boston, Chicago, Montreal, Toronto, and Minnesota."

The same may be said of the other quality leagues in baseball's minors, whose executives are pushing forward through a brave, new world. Perhaps the talent on the playing field is not up to the top-to-bottom quality of former years, as many believe, but the talent in the front office appears to be brighter than ever.

"There's no doubt that the game isn't as good as it once was, with everything being spread thin by expansion," notes McKernan. "But the minor leagues are more stable than ever because guys running the teams are better operators. I'll tell you why I say that. They have more to overcome. The guy today has to compete against television, has to compete against air conditioning. In the old days, you went to the *ballpark* to be cool. Now you've got an air-conditioned apartment, and you stay home to watch a major league game on TV. If a minor league owner can survive in today's conditions, he has to be a decent operator."

Seemingly supportive of McKernan's optimism were figures showing attendance was up in 1978.

"Some major league people would like to see the minors go away," says McKernan, "but we're a necessary evil that they must have to survive. Down deep they know they need us. That's why we'll never fold."

Here, then, are some of today's stories from that often-shadowed corner of the American sports scene. Although the following is reflective of one recent summer, the experiences and feelings are indicative of any season in the minor leagues.

1

Pride of the Yankees

The mountains lean in dramatically over left field like some spectacular Hollywood backdrop. Oh, my, it impresses. "Those," says Sam Nader proudly, "are the foothills of the Catskills." The majority stockholder of the Oneonta Yankees baseball team settles back to size up this prodigious wonder like an artist appraising his own work. "The Susquehanna River flows by here," Nader says, pointing beyond the center field fence. "The mouth is at Cooperstown, the county seat. We tell our players when they come here that this is the closest they're ever going to get to the Hall of Fame."

Twenty-two miles from Cooperstown as the baseball flies, but light years away artistically—that is the running gag in Oneonta. Still, players can dream.

"In the last ten years," Nader was saying on a brilliant summer day in 1978, "we have won five pennants and never finished lower than third. The New York Yankees have given us excellent players and we've been competitive."

If the desire to succeed is painfully intense on the Class A level of the New York-Penn League, the players at least toil in relatively serene conditions in picturesque Oneonta. Damaschke Field, a sturdy, oddly handsome ballpark, is a senior citizen among stadiums, just having edged past its seventy-fifth birthday. The eye-catching backdrop of the Catskills loom wondrously, the Yankees' own "Green Monster," but unlike the coziness of Fenway Park's legendary relic in left field, there are no easy targets at Damaschke. Only Ruthian clouts go out of the cavernous, tree-lined field.

Not only is the ballpark nestled in a splendid setting, a polished, old diamond in Oneonta's charming Neahwa Park, but the tone of play is decidedly low-key. In the New York-Penn League, they play seventy-two games a season—or less than half of a major league schedule. It is a sort of halfway house between amateurism and the pros, the first step on the long ladder to the top.

"Single-A is one of the most significant classifications for development of a ballplayer—maybe the most important one," underscores Nader. "He gets his baptism of fire, his first taste of professional ball. Whatever psychological problems there are will usually happen at this level. For that reason, and the standpoint of proper instruction, it's important as anything. If you don't build the foundation firm, the building will topple."

In Art Mazmanian, the Oneonta Yankees in 1978 had one of the most dedicated and understanding managers in all of minor league baseball, plus a coaching staff of three—unheard of at that level, or any other level for that matter, under the major leagues.

"They can say all they want about George Steinbrenner," notes Nader, his jaw firm, "but I am certainly not going to join the anvil chorus against him. He has committed himself to the minor leagues, regardless of what his public statements might be."

The general public image of the New York Yankee owner, of course, has been anything but pro-farm system, the way Steinbrenner has spent money and traded players to build his pennant-winning teams. But while Steinbrenner has been criticized for "buying" his team rather than home-growing it on the farms, the truth of the matter is that many fine players now in the majors have come up through the Yankee system—albeit now with other teams. Some of these include Cesar Geronimo, Tippy Martinez, Doc Medich, Terry Whitfield, and Dell Alston.

"They may not be on the Yankee roster," points out Nader, "but they have in fact contributed to Yankee success because they've been used in trades. People lose sight of those things."

So the Yankee farm system is planted more solidly than most people think. And Oneonta is the place where a lot of the seeds are nurtured.

A classic small town in the sense of population (16,000), Oneonta appears to be anything but average America otherwise. It is of Revolutionary War vintage and has been a home for the Fairchild aviation and camera family; one of the founders of the Union Pacific Railroad, Collis Huntingdon; and some thirty-five millionaires from IBM. It has been a source of exquisite local pride for other reasons, as well. "We used to pride ourselves on having the biggest roundhouse in the world," says Nader, a walking, talking Chamber of Commerce for the onetime railroad-oriented community. The Delaware & Hudson at one point was the biggest employer in Oneonta, but fell by the wayside with the advent of the diesel engine some fifteen years ago. "There was a lot of unemployed people then," Nader remembers, "and a cloak of pessimism covered the town. We used to have a great deal of pride in everything here, but all of a sudden the community was proud of nothing. Some people moved out during this depression of ours."

As mayor of Oneonta, Nader was in a good position to help rally the town in the problem-plagued sixties. Oneonta participated in federal programs such as urban renewal, for a start. Then came the significant ingredient of a professional baseball team. "We wanted to let the people forget the problems they thought they had," Nader says, "and let them come to the ballpark and rally 'round a team."

The Boston Red Sox established a minor league affiliate in Oneonta in 1966, but decided to pull out after only one year. This, however, did not dismay Nader—it only made him more determined to get another team. "When the Red Sox told me they were moving, you can imagine my chagrin," Nader says, "because we had upgraded the lights and had made a public announcement that the Red Sox would be back." Nader went after the franchise headfirst. "I told them to give local people a chance to buy it," says Nader, and in one hour the mayor had rounded up the necessary $10,000 to keep the team in town.

"It was an easy package to put together," explains Nader, "because I got people who were community-minded. For one particular guy, all it took was a three-minute phone call—simple as that. He didn't even care how much money was involved."

Twelve years later, the team was still firmly entrenched in town, a solid stimulus to the local economy. And Damaschke Field became a virtual community center for townspeople. The source of pride that was missing in the exasperating sixties now flowed from a baseball diamond. Everything seemed to connect after that. The college population at Hartwick exploded and the State University of New York flowered, an eye-catching campus in the so-called City of the Hills. Oneonta became a shopping center for about 120,000 people in Central New York and a perfect complement to Cooperstown as a tourist spot. "We do see a lot of tourists here," Nader says. "We have requests for baseball schedules from just about every state in the country. For the Chamber of Commerce to buy that kind of publicity, well, it would be out of this world."

The gadfly of this Oneontan renaissance is a man of substantial principles. In an always marginal franchise, Sam Nader has stuck to his ideals—even if it has meant a loss of revenue. Significantly, he has not allowed beer to be sold at Damaschke because he feels it would lead to rowdyism and discourage the family clientele. At Nader's estimate, it is a loss of $15,000 a year at the very least—but well worth it because of the climate that exists at Yankee games.

"We try to make it up on souvenirs and at the concession stands," points out Nader. "We don't lose any money. We've finished in the red only one year in the thirteen we've had the club here." But they don't make much, either, and whatever money is made by the team is put back into the product, whether it means dressing up the field or giving treats and gifts to the players. After small successes, perhaps the owner will buy pizza for the team. After large ones, the players might get parties, champagne, and rings, such as they did in the pennant-winning season of 1977.

The whole scene is an obvious labor of love for Nader, and usually it's costly labor. The New York Yankees pay salaries for the ballplayers and part of their meal money and supply uniforms—that's all. The Oneonta Athletic Corporation has to pay rent on Damaschke Field, purchase baseballs, bats and other equipment, and pay for transportation and lodging while the club is on the road. "From our standpoint," says Nader, "it probably costs us $50,000 to $75,000 a year to run the club. Overall, you'd find there's $250,000 involved in a season." The team needs a good following to help foot that kind of bill, and usually gets it. In a park that seats 3,000 comfortably ("We've had as many as 4,400 in here," says Nader), the Yankees average about 1,000 fans a game. Especially sweet was the championship season of 1977, when more than 40,000 fans attended games at Damaschke, a good figure considering that some of the thirty-six home playing dates were rained out. Promotional nights draw the biggest crowds, of course. Mickey Mantle and Joe

DiMaggio have been on hand, and the Oneonta Yankees have staged exhibition games with teams from the Triple-A International League. "We were the first ones to have a pennant night in baseball," Nader points out, "so we think we're pretty innovative."

Nader's relationship with the parent team in New York has been one good reason for his club's remarkable staying power in an unstable era of transient minor league franchises. The family spirit is evident here. "The Yankees have done everything in their power to make us content," says Nader—even to the point of remaking a roster when local fans were not happy with the quality of young men the Yankees had secured for one particular season. "One year, about three or four seasons ago, we had about fifteen players from the Caribbean countries on our team. It was difficult during that period for our townspeople to communicate with these players and I called this to the attention of the Yankees, and they corrected it. I didn't care if they were all Dominicans—we certainly are not prejudiced here. But to our fans, these ballplayers are heroes, not only with the girls, obviously, but with the old people. They like to identify with them. They take them into their homes, and when they say, 'Good morning,' they like to have them respond."

The 1978 Oneonta roster, incidentally, was still peopled with five or six athletes from South of the Border—the Yankees recognize this lush baseball fount as well as anyone else—not to mention two players from Japan. "These Japanese players are eager," Nader says, "and they're very fine men.

They hustle every minute. It's an example the American kids might do well to emulate." Haruhkiko Nakano and Fugio Tamura are part of the New York Yankees' Good Neighbor Policy with the Far East. "When Gabe Paul was with the Yankees, he made a commitment to work closely with Japanese baseball. He agreed to take some players on, to see what they could learn. Our manager is not committed to playing these kids. If we have a laugher—or a crier, as the case may be—he inserts them into the game." (Manager Art Mazmanian had to be a verbal juggler to keep up with the international mixture on his 1978 Oneonta team. "The funny thing was," he said, "I sometimes found myself talking Spanish to the Japanese players. But we eventually got that straightened out.")

One of the prides of the Oneonta Yankees this particular season was a freckled, red-haired shortstop only seventeen years old who reminded one of the character "Opie," on the old Andy Griffith show. Rex Hudler, an always-smiling, polite young man from California, looked every bit worth the reported $100,000-plus contract he got as the Yankees' number one draft choice of 1978. Hudler was batting around .300 all season and fielding with the efficacy of a big league shortshop. "A hell of an arm," an observer said. "A definite prospect."

Ted Wilborn, a svelt center fielder with wonderful range, was another. "He has a chance to play in the major leagues someday," ascertains Mazmanian. "Visiting scouts have been impressed. He was nervous and scared his first two years in pro ball, but now he's come into his own . . . he has confidence.

He can go get the ball in center field. He has a major league arm. He's an intelligent kid . . . makes few mistakes. If he hits the ball to the right of shortstop, invariably it's a hit."

The Oneonta manager was also high on Brian Dayette, a well-built youngster who played third base and also did some catching for Oneonta in 1978. "It took about two weeks of watching him and I told him, 'Brian, you're going to be the next Yankee third baseman.' Now he may be a catcher, because that's what the Yankees want to groom him for. He has a gun for an arm, and he's been our best hitter." Brian Ryder, a tall right-hander just turned eighteen, in Mazmanian's estimation "will remind people of Nolan Ryan in a year or two" and second baseman Rafael Villaman, seventeen, is "just unbelievable."

"I tell you, he's going to be a major leaguer. When we first looked at him, you thought he should have never been signed. And that's how you can be fooled. If you don't give a boy a chance to play and form a total judgment, oftentimes you leave yourself open for error. But Villaman does a lot of wonderful things. The other night, we're losing 2-1 in the seventh inning and that little guy is up there in a crouch like Pete Rose at the plate and they're almost laughing at him in the dugout. Then he hits the ball over the center field fence for a home run. He's got surprising power for a little fellow of 5-foot-9 and 150 pounds."

Although there are a few other good prospects on the Oneonta Yankees—"at least eight or nine bona fide prospects in the last two seasons," according to

Mazmanian—the manager underscores the obvious that it's still a long-shot chance for most New York-Penn League players to make it to the majors. "If you find ten bona fide prospects in the whole league in one season," he says, "that's something."

Among the NY-P graduates who made it big in the majors have been Joe Pepitone (1958 at Auburn); Phil Niekro (1959 at Wellsville); Amos Otis (1966 at Oneonta); and Cesar Geronimo (1967 at Oneonta). The Oneonta franchise has produced more than its share of big leaguers. Starting with the resurrection of a team in 1966, eighteen players graduated to the major leagues through 1977 from the proud Central New York community, certifying the Yankees as one of the top producers of farm crops.

It is a classic grass-roots setting which serves as the stage for development of young talent. Major league barnstormers once made Oneonta one of the stops on their tours. Such as Babe Ruth, Rogers Hornsby, and Christy Mathewson graced the Oneonta ballpark. Ed Moore, a local historian, remembered when the visiting stars dressed in the old YMCA on Broad Street and the kids would wait outside the building to carry the ballplayers' gloves and equipment to the park. "I carried Christy Mathewson's glove once all over the town," Moore related. "My feet never touched the ground once."

It wasn't called Damaschke Field then, but Neahwa Park, a name generally given to the entire recreation area nowadays. The field received its present name in 1968 in honor of E. C. "Dutch"

Damaschke, chairman of the Parks and Recreation Committee for Oneonta.

The field had its start in 1903 when Louis R. Morris, a descendant of the family for which the Otsego County Village of Morris is named, gave the land to Oneonta. Back then, the field was called Elm Park by the many semipro and amateur teams that played there, one of them a colorful aggregation called the Blue Label Cigars. "Apparently," pointed out an observer, "the name comes from the fact that many elm trees graced the park." They still do.

Players from Brown University, Holy Cross, Syracuse, and Williams College played ball in the summers in Oneonta from around the 1910–1912 period. The playing field, at one time reputed to be the largest playing area of any park anywhere except old Forbes Field in Pittsburgh, served as a stamping ground for various football teams as well as dog and horse shows and track meets. The Oneonta Giants of the old New York-Penn League played there in the twenties and Oneonta's entry in the Canadian American League occupied the ballpark in the thirties and forties. Pro baseball was absent from Damaschke from 1950 to 1966 until the new NY-P League established a Red Sox team there.

Legends still persist of Ruth's Herculean homers. He hit them when Damaschke Field was a good deal larger than it is now. But according to Moore, a player by the name of Austin J. Knickerbocker hit one of the longest balls he ever saw hit at Damaschke. He played in the Cam-Am League around the 1940s.

"Knickerbocker was a good player," said Moore. "He hit .404 one season and could play shortstop, left field, third base as well as pitch."

Damaschke Field could hold more people then, Moore remembered. "Crowds of 4,000 and 5,000 were not uncommon." Lights came to Damaschke during the Can-Am days and many improvements in the lighting system have made it one of the best in Class A ball.

The league in which the Oneonta Yankees play ties in with some significant baseball history. Originally it was called the P.O.N.Y. League (Pennsylvania, Ontario, New York) before a spinoff resulted in the Eastern League and New York-Penn League in the 1940s. The NY-P League was founded in 1948 and managed to survive as one of the oldest continuous minor league organizations in the country. It has been a persistent group, considering the change of climate in the minor league system through the years.

Ironically, the New York-Penn League no longer has a team from Pennsylvania in it—the last one was Williamsport, which recently relocated in Elmira, a Boston Red Sox farm team. Along with Oneonta and Elmira, the other NY-P teams are Utica, Auburn, Little Falls, Geneva, Jamestown, Batavia, Newark, and Niagara Falls. "We decided to keep the name, even though we didn't have a Pennsylvania team in the league, because we thought historically it meant something," says Sam Nader. "And perhaps some time we will have a Pennsylvania team back in."

The survival of the league is simple enough to explain, according to Nader: "We treat our teams like our family. Most of the clubs in this league are comprised similar to our organization—we're doing it from the community standpoint."

Oneonta might be considered the jewel of this legendary league—cosmetically, at least. This bucolic town is embraced by a timeless, quiet beauty. Circling into town on soft, rolling mountain roads, one is struck by a classic panorama—Oneonta nestled at the bottom in a picture-card setting, glazed by summer. The mountains, the most prominent feature of the place, arch against a high sky, and form an awe-inspiring backdrop. You can walk to anyplace that is meaningful in town and on a typical small town Main Street (actually, that is the name), a banner with red lettering on a white background hangs overhead announcing that this is the "Home of the Oneonta Yankees." It is certainly a conversation piece for everyone from the customers in the popular Diana Restaurant to the room clerks at the Town House Motel.

"Damaschke Field is a good place for people to go on a summer night," points out Elizabeth Harrington, a senior citizen who works at the Town House during the day and is a big fan of the Oneonta Yankees at night. "It's a social meeting place—sort of like a community center."

Mrs. Harrington has been a fixture in the stands behind home plate at Damaschke for quite a few years now, forming a tight triumverate with two other passionate fans, Mrs. Isabel McManus and Miss Lu Beers. All in their seventies, they can be seen at just about every home game the Yankees play, keeping box scores with the precision and care of a veteran sportswriter and eating hot dogs and popcorn with the abandon of youth. If anyone must be considered the unofficial number one fan of the Oneonta Yankees, Mrs. McManus wears that title with distinction. "She gave the Yankees a check one year when they had a bad season," remembers Mrs. Harrington. Baseball has been a big part of Mrs. McManus's life. She has several scrapbooks filled with clippings on the Oneonta Yankees, possesses one of the world's biggest collections of New York Yankee yearbooks, and has had Oneonta players stay in her house over the summer.

"You develop emotional ties with these players," said Mrs. Harrington, "and it just tears you up to see them leave. But Isabel has kept in contact with some of them."

The tight relationship with the players in Oneonta is not uncommon on that minor league level, yet Mrs. Harrington likes to think: "This is more friendly than a lot of other places. Also, I think we might be more baseball-minded than other communities because we're so near Cooperstown. This might not be your average minor league town at all."

Indicative of the community spirit that has grown with the baseball team was a petition signed by townspeople not long ago against a proposed city rent increase on Damaschke Field. The increase never went through.

The most appealing quality of minor league baseball—intimacy—is never more apparent than at Damaschke. The Oneonta players dress in a mobile home·unit set up behind the stands at home plate, then mingle with the fans and even get refreshments at the concession stand. The scene has the conviviality of a college affair, down to the climate of the fans. Oneontans cheer everything, even acknowledging great performances by visiting teams.

"The fans rarely get on the local players," says Bob Whittemore, a longtime Oneonta sportswriter. "They may go through a season and never get booed. It's a happy situation. The kids for the most part are comfortable here."

Whittemore, now removed from the Oneonta sports scene after assuming the stewardship of a newspaper upstate, was back in his familiar spot behind home plate at Damaschke Field one summer night of 1978—this time, as a fan. Expounding on his favorite subject while Brian Ryder was throwing a strong game for Oneonta, Whittemore reflected: "Most of these players here will never play big league baseball—a sad truism if ever there was one. But they will carry with them experiences which will be with them always. Small solace when you get the word you're through, but an important factor in future life nevertheless."

Most of the athletes Whittemore knew in his association with the Oneonta Yankees had professional situations developing "on the outside" as a safeguard against baseball failure. Players in leagues such as the NY-P, in fact, might sign "college clause" contracts which enable them to continue their educations, usually at club expense. "Most give themselves about three, four years to make it in baseball," says Whittemore.

Dreams die hard, though. There have been hundreds such as Ingram "Arch" Haley, who had been told one fateful summer day by the Oneonta Yankees that he had been released. Haley went back to the clubhouse to fight back tears—he was twenty-three. Then he said: "I have an education. I have a teaching job waiting for me. Financially, I'm going to be okay. But don't you see, I've been an athlete all my life and this is the first time I didn't make the team. I didn't make the team . . ."

Others know themselves when it is time to quit. "Walt Peto was a great little second baseman of the early days," Whittemore remembers. "Walt had a little baby and another on the way. He was sent to Oneonta for the third straight year. He was here only a few hours before he said, 'No way. I'm a family man now with responsibilities. For me to stay in Class A another day would be foolish . . . and unfair. I guess this is it.'"

Some don't mind even tougher odds—such as Andy Bottin. "A big, warm, lovable kid," according to Whittemore, Bottin signed at a young age and played in Oneonta for a season before serving in Vietnam. There, he suffered ghastly wounds while saving a buddy. He came back to Oneonta after his Army service, but his war-torn legs couldn't deliver what his spirit asked. Recalls Whittemore: "Manager George Case one night in Williamsport near the end of the season said he had never seen a kid he had wanted to make it more than Andy . . . but it just wasn't there."

Some are far more nonchalant. "Boom Boom" Crowder, a colorful Canadian who remained in

Oneonta for a couple of years, was of this variety. The happy-go-lucky Crowder knew he wasn't headed for Yankee Stadium, but he didn't seem to care. Crowder told a reporter one day about his "discovery" by a Yankee scout: "Hey, this dude comes up out of the brush one day up in Saskatchewan where I'm a pitcher. He gives me $500 for my signature, I sign, and here I am—a pitcher." That, of course, was debatable. At one time his earned-run average hit 37.900—a dubious record for Oneonta pitchers.

Ryder, the tall, slim right-hander whom Manager Art Mazmanian had described as a future Nolan Ryan, is certainly not of Crowder's ilk. Struggling a bit in the early innings against the Elmira Red Sox, he rights himself and holds the visitors to one run and two hits in seven innings. The Yankees eventually win, 10-3, as Wilborn and Villaman, two of the players that Mazmanian admires, each knock in two runs. The family feeling on the Yankees is expressed in the second inning when the entire Oneonta team comes out to greet Matt Winters at home plate after the big outfielder hits a home run over the distant right field fence.

"Of course it isn't the easiest life in the world, playing in the minors," Whittemore says in between shouts of encouragement for the home team. "The kids don't sleep right, and they don't eat right. It used to drive George Case nuts to see his players eat potato chips and coke for breakfast. 'I never heard of such a thing,' George would say. The Oneonta players all got sick eating fish sandwiches one time at Jamestown and came back, throwing up all over the place. They really looked sick when they played, too, and the fans really booed 'em. But eating has to be a real problem. The kids have to be at the ballpark usually around five o'clock, sometimes earlier. And they get out at eleven, or maybe even later. It's hard to find a restaurant around here that's open that time of night. It seems they're always hungry.

"And the bus rides, well, they're unbelievable. Jamestown to Oneonta is six hours, but it would be all right if the roads were good. But the bus swings and rocks a lot, and you can't sleep. I went on a road trip once with the team and came back so tired I couldn't believe it." (Although the trip to Niagara Falls is farther it is an easier one, Whittemore says, because the road is a superhighway most of the way. The ride smoother, players are able to sleep, many of them settling into the luggage racks above the seats.)

Along with the lack of food and sleep and the painfully long bus rides, there are other unpleasant surprises along the minor league trail.

"When Frank Verdi was managing here," Whittemore says, "he took the team to Batavia one day for a scheduled single game and found out that it had suddenly become a doubleheader. That really made Verdi mad and he refused to play two games. So the Yankees went home after the first game. The league President, Vince McNamara, called to fine Verdi, and Frank really gave him an earful. He refused to accept the fine, just as he had refused to play that doubleheader. 'You little s. o. b.' Verdi told McNamara, 'you couldn't fine me $200 if you were President of the United States.'"

One of the charms of minor league baseball, the distinction of the parks, leads to another Whittemore story.

"Auburn has a field which is about 225 feet down the right field line and an infield pop fly sometimes turns into a home run down there. Well, Oneonta had a player named Brian Engle in the late 1960s who hit one off his fists and the ball just squeezed over that short fence for a homer. Brian just stood at home plate, amazed to see the ball go over the fence. Really, he didn't move. Finally, Manager Jerry Walker screams out, 'Brian, trot.' And Engle, not known to hit home runs, fires back: 'But, skipper, I don't have a home run trot.' "

Auburn, by the way, was not always one of Whittemore's favorite stops when he was a sportswriter.

"They used to have to kill rats before they could get into the dressing room there. And, after nine showers, there was no hot water left."

Life in the minors is sometimes just as tough on radio broadcasters as it is on players. Whittemore, who occasionally pinch-hit as an announcer for WGNR ("Good News Radio"), had a technical problem once while broadcasting Oneonta's game at Niagara Falls. He had gone down to the park early to make sure that his hookup with the station was working, but instead found it dead. He wound up doing the game over a special telephone hookup, but it wasn't comfortable. "The wire was short and I had to do fourteen innings on my knees," he says.

That couldn't have been any more embarrassing

than what happened one night to Eddie Lyons, a manager for the Erie ballclub.

"Lyons had a hot date and made a deal with umpire Ross Cruscilla to get thrown out of the game early. Well, when Lyons came out to raise some hell, Cruscilla took his cue and sent him to the showers. But long about the eighth inning, Cruscilla looks up in the stands behind home plate and sees Lyons sitting there. Lyons told him afterward: 'I tried to get out but my car was blocked.' So it cost him $50 for nothing."

2

On a Clear Day You Can See New York

Jersey City's boast to baseball fame these days is largely historical, housing a museum piece of a ballpark in Roosevelt Stadium, a home plateful of golden memories and little recognizable local pride. Once it was the Rome of a gaudy minor league world. In their glory days, the Jersey City Giants produced such major league demigods as Bobby Thomson, Sal Maglie, Monte Irvin, and Whitey Lockman, and once-vital Roosevelt Stadium thundered with the sound and fury of enraptured fans. Now the mosquitos usually outnumber the customers in this patriarch of baseball parks, while the apathy and weeds grow around. It hasn't been easy trying to resurrect professional baseball in a virtual ghost town.

"At times it's depressing when you see just eighty people in the ballpark," says Arnie Reichbaum, a rail-thin, eager young man with an Afro hairdo who was director of operations for the Jersey Indians in 1978. "You have to wonder if the interest would be better if we were connected with the New York Yankees."

This lack of local identity cost the Indians somewhat in their second season as an Eastern League member in Jersey City. They were caught up in a fairly common geographical irony of the minors—that is, an affiliation with a major league team which is based thousands of miles away. In this case, the Oakland A's. The team was with Cleveland the year before, and retained the nickname "Indians" even though cutting ties with the parent club. There had been overtures to bring the Yankees into Jersey City to direct the Class AA team, but nothing had materialized in Reichbaum's second year with the team, a twist of fate he bemoaned.

"If we got the Yankees in here—or even the New York Mets—we could get 1,000 a night," Reichbaum said one shining summer day as he watched the Indians take batting practice. "I've seen pictures where this stadium was filled, where people were sitting along the fence out there. Maybe we wouldn't do that again, but at least we could get respectable crowds in here. The Yankees could do a lot of things publicity-wise for us. They could advertise on their scoreboard at the Stadium, possibly have an exhibition game with the farm club here . . . and it would be completely different."

More significantly, the Jersey City fans would be able to identify with local heroes on the way up. The A's, logically, drafted most of their players from California—75 percent, by Reichbaum's arithmetic. "We don't have one player from Jersey, let alone the

East Coast," he said with a grimace.

New franchises traditionally trigger an explosion of interest in town, but the Indians seemed cursed from the start of their arrival in Jersey City in 1977. Transplanted from Williamsport, Pa., and headed by a team of rich New York businessmen and an outspoken, hard-driving general manager in Mal Fichman, the club hardly got settled before feeling ill winds. Fichman, never one to keep his thoughts to himself, complained loudly that the response from Jersey City business and industry was terrible. He said that many of the politicians involved in bringing the team to Jersey City did little to support it after the season started. "There were people in Jersey City who were predicting and perhaps even hoping for the Jersey City franchise to fail," said one sportswriter. An enraged Fichman charged that the city was not adhering to parts of its lease agreement on Roosevelt Stadium, and obviously this did not endear him to Jersey City Mayor Thomas F. X. Smith. There was bad feeling between the two and at some low points in their relationship, even a Kissinger would have had problems making peace. As it turned out, peace was never made between the two.

Further, Fichman was blamed for putting together a sorrowful team, hardly inspiring public confidence with a 39-96 record in his first year. Always in the eye of the hurricane, Fichman was not exactly the newspaperman's friend, either. He belabored the point of poor media coverage, yet did little to provide assistance for writers. As Mike Spina pointed out in the *Hudson Dispatch:* "Maybe more of the media would have attended if games had started earlier or the team had rented the machinery to transmit stories directly to a paper. The general manager complained of being treated like a semipro team when, in effect, he could have made the team a professional outfit by renting the necessary machinery for the papers. At one point early in the season, the invisible PR stat sheet failed to provide a numbered roster to identify the team's players. Team statistics of the visiting team were never provided in full."

Fichman further offended the newspapers' sensibilities, and hurt credibility, by padding attendance figures. The Eastern League record crowd of 8,800 for one game was said to be closer to 4,000 by some observers. At one point during the frustrating 1977 season, when an approximate crowd of 4,000 showed up, the team, according to one reporter, was considering releasing an attendance figure of 8,000 since it was a major promotional night.

But even with all this, perhaps the alienation could have changed to affection had Fichman adhered more closely to the area of public relations and promotion. Press conferences became a farce, when after the early part of the season, they were called in an urgent manner and then revealed little of material use. After awhile, most reporters stopped showing up. Not once during the 1977 season did the Indians make a push into the lucrative North Hudson area to try to attract fans to Roosevelt Stadium. And when a clinic for Little League teams was held at the Stadium, admission was charged for the participants—markedly alienating the public. "Fichman's first mistake," said one observer, "was in not hiring a full-time public relations man."

That oversight was corrected in 1978 when a media coordinator was hired to travel with the team and dispense information and game stories to local papers. "Publicity has picked up," noted Reichbaum. "It may not show in the attendance, but it has. The problem is just that not enough people know that there's a team in Jersey City."

That was never the case back in the 1930s and 1940s, of course, when minor league baseball was king in New Jersey. The state supported not one—but two—teams, the Jersey City Giants and the Newark Bears of the Triple-A International League. And these teams were a source of pride to their communities. The attendance reflected this intense feeling, sometimes surpassing that of their major league counterparts across the river—the Yankees, New York Giants, and Brooklyn Dodgers. For one opening day game with the Rochester Red Wings, 36,234 tickets were sold to virtually split the sides of Roosevelt Stadium. The park seated only 25,000. In 1941, more than 56,000 tickets were sold for a game in which, luckily, only 45,000 showed up. During these years, the Jersey City club played under the aegis of Mayor Frank ("I Am the Law") Hague, who reputedly could sell an anchor to a drowning man. Boss Hague made about $6,000 a year in salary, but owned a $125,000 estate in Florida and seemed to live like royalty. "Good investments," was his reply to the perennial question of his luxurious life-style.

Hague is an important name in Jersey City baseball history for it was he who had Roosevelt

Stadium built, put up in 1937 with some $3 million of W. P. A. (Works Progress Administration) funds. It was a handsome art deco structure with a glass, brick, and wrought-iron facade. Perhaps not exactly of major league caliber, it was a virtual palace for a minor league team. Fans didn't seem to mind that there were no permanent box seats, only folding chairs. During Roosevelt Stadium's maiden season, 233,370 people flocked to the House That Hague Built.

On April 18, 1946, Jersey City became the birthplace of integration in organized baseball when a twenty-eight-year-old infielder name Jackie Robinson made his professional debut with the Montreal Royals. "They threw a black cat on the field and booed him," recalled Al Keenan, the Roosevelt Stadium superintendent. "Then he got three singles and a home run, scored four runs, drove in four, and stole two bases. In the end, they gave him a standing ovation." Robinson returned to Jersey City with the Brooklyn team when the Dodgers played seven of their regular-season games in Roosevelt Stadium in 1956. In 1960 and 1961 the Havana Sugar Kings, refugees from Fidel Castro's Cuba, made their home in Jersey City, then quietly disappeared, and then Roosevelt Stadium lay fallow for sixteen seasons before the Indians came to town in 1977.

Jersey City's big hits not only include integration, but the advent of big-time night games. Once during the 1920s, the Donnelly family, which operated the franchise, lured fans to now-razed West Side Park by staging a night game. "We rented kliegs from the Majestic Light Company," noted Frank Donnelly, the team's general manager. "But the lighting was only so-so, and we couldn't stay with it. The score of that game was something like 11-0. It was burlesque." But it was still light years ahead of the major leagues, which did not play a night game until 1935, at Cincinnati.

Other historical gems abound in Jersey City's rich baseball lore. Before Robinson made his dramatic splash, another black player cut out some history for himself sixty years before in the heavily industrialized community. George Stovey, a pitcher who won thirty-five games for Jersey City in 1886, reportedly was the first black to play in pro baseball. Jersey City has had minor league baseball teams intermittently since 1878. Before harvesting splendid talents for the New York Giants in the 1930s and 1940s, Jersey City grew beautiful crops of big-league players. Among them were Lefty Grove, Bobo Newsome, Babe Herman, Dixie Walker, and George "Twinkletoes" Selkirk, Babe Ruth's replacement who was nicknamed after a Jersey City showgirl.

All of these bright names, and many more major leaguers, grew up under the auspices of the Donnellys, long considered the First Family of baseball in Jersey City, and set the foundation for the glory days of Mayor Hague. It's quite possible, though, that neither the Donnellys nor Hague would have recognized opening day 1977, at Roosevelt Stadium. For one thing, it was opening night. For another, only 1,643 fans showed up. And for another, the Indians lost a 3-2, ten-inning decision to the Bristol

Red Sox, a circumstance usually alien to the old Jersey City franchise.

The ballpark had deteriorated as well, "to a point where it was disgraceful," said one writer. "The rest rooms resembled the community pool, with about six inches of water on the floor. There were no lights in the ramps leading to the stands, and the scoreboard looked like a leftover from the thirties—which it was."

Meanwhile, with the Indians losing consistently in their first year in Jersey City, the town of Mt. Vernon, N. Y., signed them to play an exhibition game there June 4, and made overtures to move the team there permanently. Fichman even admitted there was a "fifty-fifty chance" that his club would move to the town in New York State, and this of course did nothing to help attendance in Jersey City. By the end of the season, the Indians had the dubious distinction of the worst record in baseball and a king-size inferiority complex. On the surface, the reasons seemed clear for failure—a pathetic team playing in an archaic stadium. But the problems were deeper than that.

Many fans complained about the lack of public transportation to the ballpark. "The city was supposed to supply busses from Journal Square," said Reichbaum, "but nothing ever came of it." The team complained of the lack of media respect. "The press was terrible," said one club official. "They didn't cover any games. If they had room, they would do us a favor and put in a paragraph at the bottom of the page." The complacency of the fans was believed to be another factor for the first-year frustrations. "The people of Jersey City just have a bad attitude," noted Afraim Morales, the team's ticket manager. "They really aren't sports-minded. All they care about are the Yankee scores."

Unappreciative of the situation, the Cleveland Indians set out to find a new minor league affiliate. The Oakland A's, looking for a Double-A team, moved in for the 1978 season and Fichman wasted little time in securing a new manager and signing some precocious players. In John Kennedy, Fichman had a well-known and well-traveled former major league infielder and a manager of some success. The first player that Fichman signed was a young outfielder with a seemingly bright future named Ricky Henderson. Playing in 1977 for Modesto in the California league, Henderson hit .345 and stole a spectacular ninety-five bases. In 1978, he was predictably among the base-stealing leaders of the Eastern League. The Indians later came up with another gem in Daryl Woodward, a second baseman who like Henderson could steal bases and hit with authority. Around the nucleus of these two players, the Indians built a better team in 1978, and also better relations with the city.

Thanks to a federal grant, the stadium finally got a well-deserved face-lift. The lights were improved (although some complain that they are still among the worst in Double-A baseball), the plumbing problems were cleaned up, and the choice seats were painted and refurbished. Only the stone bleacher seats along the left- and right-field lines, one of the few eyesores in the place, were left untouched. Thus, about half of the 25,000-odd seats were usable for the 1978 season, a pretty composition of red, white, and blue sections. The renovations even included a new press box to appease the newspapermen and from which Reichbaum proudly proclaims, "On a clear day, you can see the New York skyline."

Perhaps one of the most important steps taken was the one to sign what amounted to a peace treaty with City Hall. This was symbolically summed up in the lease for 1978. According to Mayoral Aide Frank Roberts, the previous year's lease was a "giveaway operation of the previous administration." Roberts said that the city lost about $120,000 on the stadium in 1977. Under terms of the new lease, the city got a higher percentage of concessions, outfield advertising, souvenir and scorecard sales, and admissions. The rental of the stadium was increased from $6,000 to $15,000 a year. (Even with the supposed good deal that the Indians got on the Roosevelt Stadium lease in 1977, it is interesting to note that the team lost a "significant amount" of money that year, according to one of the owners, Joseph Rosenberg.)

The owners have to put up about $150,000 a year to sustain the franchise, and according to one high Eastern League observer, Rosenberg and his group can handle that. ("There's a lot of money there.") But, overwhelmed by the Yankees, Mets, and TV, they have been swimming in a sea of red ink thus far, hoping for a life raft from the fans. In this regard, Reichbaum and his energetic front-office crew worked hard at promotional schemes in 1978, inviting organizations and businesses to sponsor special days. One night, former pitching ace Bob Feller came in to give a clinic, although it was not as successful as Reichbaum would have liked. "It was a dreary day," said the director of operations, "and we only had 1,000 in the park. They were expecting more, but I guess considering the weather, it was a pretty good turnout." There were some good crowds at Roosevelt Stadium, including 6,000 on an "All-School Night," but only because the Board of Education helped distribute free tickets to school-age youngsters. For the most part, an average night's attendance in 1978 was in the undistinguished neighborhood of 300 to 400, and for one forgettable game featured a two-year low of 82 at Roosevelt Stadium. "That," said Reichbaum, "was certainly depressing."

On a windless summer night, a family of five tooled up Route 440, past a sign that said, "Bayonne —Keep Right," to find a new relationship with minor league baseball. The head of this clan, after all, had been fed major league quality from birth and now would find another beauty in the minors—the wonderful intimacies and frailties which are the mark of that caliber of professionalism. A restaurant called "The Timbers" advertised "Disco" and "Greek Night—Belly Dancer," the Hudson Mall loomed on the right, followed by stacks of factories. A hot orange sun was sinking in the sky directly behind the Baldwin Steel plant. A small sign with the word "Stadium" turned off into the road circling the home of the Jersey Indians, hard by unspectacular

Newark Bay. Chuck Hockenberry, a bespectacled right-hander who had just come down from the A's Triple-A team in Vancouver, was pitching this night against the Reading Phillies, one of the better teams in the Eastern League, and a long layover from his last start was evident in his lack of control. In the early going, Hockenberry hits a batter and throws a wild pitch. He is betrayed more, though, by his fielders, who make four errors in the first four innings, and one of these leads to a Reading run.

The stands are quiet, as the Indians toil before a meager crowd estimated at less than 200, and individual conversations can be heard—as well as those on the field. Once, the Jersey manager bawls out an umpire after a close play at first that completed a double play against his team. "At least be near the goddamn bag when you call the play!" Kennedy shouts from the dugout in a deep bass that thunders to the cavernous outer reaches of the huge stadium. When a Reading player throws a bat at a pitch, one fan is heard to say: "You can't get to the majors that way!" And during one period when Hockenberry continues to throw over to first base to keep a fidgety runner close, someone says: "That's it—keep dirtying his uniform!"

Ron McNeely of the Indians makes a wonderful catch against the fence in left to save a run for Jersey and shortly thereafter, the lights go out in the stadium. "It isn't only us," points out a beleagured Reichbaum, "the whole area is blacked out."

It is bad enough for people sitting in the stands, but fans caught in the concession area during the

blackout are completely in the dark, literally and fig-
uratively speaking. "Christ!" flares one, "I just lost
my soda and pretzels." "Watch out for looters,"
screams another.

An auxiliary power source is used, and one by one
the light standards begin to blaze again with their
old authority amid strained remarks of disturbed
fans. "Strike two," a voice says, making a weak joke
about using matches instead of lights. The lights
soon die again. This happens more than once, accompanied by groans and caustic remarks. Finally,
they are on to stay—except for one stubborn light
standard near home plate. The players, meanwhile,
stay around the field in clusters, playing games of
pepper and chatting animately. Some players settle
on top of the dugouts and youngsters come over to
sit with them, talk, and get autographs.

"This isn't unusual," Greg Cochran, one of the
leading pitchers on the Jersey staff, tells a fan sitting
behind home plate. "It happened to me last year at
Chattanooga."

Soon enough, the game is suspended. "We can't
turn on that last light standard, or we'll blow out
everything again," explains an engineer.

The Night the Lights Went Out at Roosevelt Stadium—apropos, one might think, of the trouble-
some rebirth of baseball in Jersey City.

"Life in the minors," sighs a dispirited
Reichbaum, "that's the way it is."

3

PawSox and More Sox

The state of Rhode Island has irreplaceable Newport, one of the true beauties of the country, and a coastline that can often break your heart. But Pawtucket (pronounced Pah-tucket by most of the natives) is not especially a place frequented by the Beautiful People. One look at the blue-collar neighborhoods and shopping areas will tell you what the purchasing power of the community is. "It is not," says Ben Mondor, "the most affluent place in the world. Cultural life is suffering. The libraries are going down and the repertory company here staggers from one life-surviving drive to another."

This, however, did not stop Mondor from investing in baseball there. The vibrant owner of the Pawtucket Red Sox had a dream.

"When I took over this franchise in 1976," he says, "this place was the pits. The team was in a bankrupt state that nobody wanted. I mean, there were hundreds of thousands of dollars worth of debts here. Plus the stadium had a bad reputation. There was plenty of vandalism—kids breaking up cars and running loose around the stadium throwing hot dogs full of mustard at people. . ."

Mondor instituted a get-tough policy the first night the Red Sox were in town under his aegis. He had plenty of muscle in McCoy Stadium, with a bunch of Pinkerton guards and policemen, and Mondor remembers: "That first night, we put out something like 135 people. The next night we put out maybe ten—and then, we didn't have any more trouble after that."

Made safe for the family trade, and accompanied by good family prices, McCoy Stadium suddenly became a beautifully sane place on summer nights. The crowds began to come, as Mondor had predicted, and by the end of the 1977 season the so-called PawSox were averaging 1,200 a game. That was the figure Mondor had been shooting for in his passionate preseason hopes.

The honky-tonk atmosphere of previous seasons was gone, thanks to Mondor. Gimmicks were out and promotionals held to a minimum, and the ebullient owner was fervently satisfied with his first-year's product. Others were amazed.

"Everyone said it couldn't be done," says Mondor. "But we were doing it. I sell one thing here—and that's pure professional baseball. That's all I'll ever sell."

Apparently the word got out fast enough to the public, because 1978 became a banner year for the PawSox. Near the end of the season, Mondor's International League team was well over the 100,000 mark in attendance—or nearly 2,000 a game!

"We made it pleasant and inexpensive to go to a

ballgame," points out Mondor. "With a ten-dollar bill, you and your wife and kids can come in, have a couple of beers and hot dogs and coke, and everything else, and go home with a dollar change."

At McCoy, they charge three dollars for box seats, two dollars for general admission, one dollar for senior citizens, and half-price for children under twelve. At the concession stands, soda is thirty-five cents, hot dogs fifty cents, and beer sixty. "These are things that are seventy-five cents, eighty-five cents, and a dollar in other places," notes Mondor, then adds almost apologetically: "Popcorn, we brought up from twenty-five cents to fifty. But the reason we did it was because we more than doubled the size of the box. It's made right here. If we followed the other parks, we would charge the traditional seventy-five cents."

Parking is free at this neighborly ballpark, along with the friendly greetings from concessionaires—a warmth that seems to filter down from the owner. Notes Ed Bridges, a writer for the Enterprise-Sun Newspapers, Inc.: "When I visited the refreshment stand, the vendor in charge greeted me like an old friend instead of like somebody who had come to do him wrong or who should be shortchanged as quickly as possible and sent on his way."

Mondor, a dynamo of a man who rarely seems to rest, is personally responsible for all this familial feeling. He stalks the stands during games, playfully wrestling with his employees or chatting with fans. His feverish hospitality is catching. "Ben Mondor is a fantastic owner to work for," concludes Mike Tamburro, the Pawtucket general manager. "He didn't want to hype the team the way it was in the past with assorted gimmicks that made the product seem like a carnival act. He just wants to sell baseball, be a professional. And, he's a lovely human being."

For the fans, the way into venerable McCoy Stadium is made easy and pleasurable—in Mondor's words, "no hassle." You can usually find a spot in the spacious parking lot and buy a ticket at the front gate with a pleasant word or two from the man behind the wicket before heading up the ramps. The ramps! Now, *those* are conversation pieces, all right. Mondor has a virtual fetish about his players and once they make the major leagues, he honors them by having the player's mural emblazoned on the wall in full color along the ramp to the main gate. It is an eye-catching outdoor museum.

Along with those rich-looking murals, McCoy Stadium is endowed with a special elegance. This cream-colored colossus is of a grand, classic design, one of the sturdiest and handsomest of minor league stadiums. From the outside, it looks much larger than it is, mainly because of its massive concrete structure. The seats are of one flowing tier and grouped mostly between the first- and third-base lines, and a visitor is flabbergasted when the owner reports a capacity of only 6,500. "It looks much larger, doesn't it?" Mondor says, smiling. "Everyone says that." Conveniently, a roof covers all the seats—practically a necessity in the inconsistent New England summer weather.

Built in 1942 in the swamps and quicksand of

Hammond Pond, McCoy Stadium cost $1.5 million to construct, making it the most expensive stadium in America at the time—even more expensive than Notre Dame's stadium with its 59,000 seats or Ohio State's 80,000-seat monster in Columbus.

So the atmosphere is good. And the red, white, blue, or gold seats are close enough to the field so that you can hear Pawtucket Manager Joe Morgan bait the umpires. ("I don't give a living bleep what you saw; the ball was foul, and you know it.") When catcher Gary Allenson shouts to his infield, or second baseman Buddy Hunter talks it up, it can be clearly heard. The resonant crack of the bat is sharper, it seems, because of the intimacy of the place.

"Everything was very homey," Ed Bridges once wrote of his first visit to McCoy. "The home plate umpire was from Watertown. Whenever things got dull we could yell, 'Go back to Watertown' at him. And he took it all in friendly fashion, waving and winking between innings. They don't act that way at Shea Stadium or Fenway Park, by golly."

From high in the press box that hangs out of the roof behind home plate, Mike Pappas, the congenial public address announcer, intones the players' names with a striking clarity. He is a sometime disc jockey as well, playing such diverse melodies as the theme from *Rocky,* songs from *Saturday Night Fever,* or the western tune, *Thank God I'm a Country Boy*. Then he intermittently offers cases of coke or free tickets for such intriguing baseball questions as, "Who did Don Larson strike out for the last out of his perfect game in the 1956 World Series? And who was the losing pitcher?"

The players' wives are always grouped together in the gold seats just to the left of home plate, some doing double-duty as baby nurses and cheerleaders.

"My baby's on a baseball schedule," says Anita Coleman, wife of outfielder Dave Coleman. "She's trained to go to sleep at eleven p. m. It doesn't seem to bother her at all."

Actually, balancing babies and baseball is the least of Anita Coleman's worries. It's a lot tougher following her husband as his career bounces up and down.

"He spent a short time with Boston," Mrs. Coleman says, "when Carl Yastrzemski didn't feel like facing Frank Tanana and Vida Blue. Dave didn't strike out. He didn't disgrace himself. But when they sent him down, they cut his salary to the minor league level again. That was the first time the Red Sox had done that in ten years. It was lousy."

The toughest part of the game for Mrs. Coleman is loneliness. "I dread the times the team goes on the road, and I have to wait for Dave to come back."

Hanky Bowen undoubtedly spent more time with her husband, Sam, at Valdosta State College in Georgia than she has in her 2 ½ years of marriage.

"I was the team bat girl at Valdosta, so I traveled with him through his college career," notes the wife of the Pawtucket center fielder. "But then I taught special education back home, and of course Sam played professional baseball. It was tough, but I guess it's just the price you have to pay for our careers. I figure we've been apart a year of those 2½ years."

Second baseman Buddy Hunter's wife, Lori, is a veteran baseball wife who seems to have adjusted to the eccentricities of that position. At thirty-one, her husband is the oldest of the Pawtucket players and that makes Lori the unofficial leader of the sorority set. "I love the excitement, the travel, meeting people," she says, brightly. "The only tough thing for me is getting settled at the start of the year."

The girls spend much of their time together, shopping, sightseeing, going to the movies, and waiting— waiting for the scores on the evening news, for the stories in the morning newspapers, for the bus to arrive at McCoy Stadium with their husbands.

"They're great people," says Murray Friedman, head of the Pawtucket Red Sox Boosters Club. "When we first met them, we used to call the wives 'The Cutsies.' But after we got to know them, we found that they were not only good-looking, but nice, bright gals as well. We've loved them all."

That, of course, is another problem of minor league life: making friends one season, and losing them the next.

"The best thing we could wish the wives is that we hope not to see them again next year," says Friedman's wife, Cathy. "That means it's a step up for them. We develop emotional attachments with these people—and they leave. That's the hardest part for us. But that's the way it is."

If the relationships are short-lived, they are at least intense. Friedman personally sees to that in the

Booster Club. Among other things, the club arranges to have players visit local homes for get-togethers, inspiring a feeling of acceptance for the player and a feeling of intimacy for the fan. Friedman, supervisor of a children's institution in nearby Providence, understands perhaps better than most the significance of human relationships and thus works especially hard at this aspect of his Booster Club duties. His attempts at matching players with households have hit the mark on more than one occasion, as it did once with Win Remmerswaal. In order to make the pitcher from Holland feel more at home, a countryman who spoke only Dutch was brought over the house and, except for getting a flat tire that night, Remmerswaal had a memorable evening.

The Booster Club is an integral part of Pawtucket baseball these days. Started in 1977 with Ben Mondor's blessing, the club sponsors pregame picnics in a grassy area along the left-field line at McCoy Stadium, encouraging a wholesome, family trade. Appealing even more to families, perhaps, are the prices for games. Once a member of the club, you can see the Pawtucket Red Sox play for half-price, whether the seat be a box or general admission.

The Booster Club would seem to be a direct extension of Mondor's thinking.

"I don't ask for much," he says. "I want this to be a place where the fans can come out with their families and watch good baseball and have a good time."

Mondor doesn't use the term "good baseball"

loosely. "I honestly think that this is better than the major leagues," he says, "because the players here are trying harder to make it. The guy upstairs might have a five-year, $2-million contract, and half the money's in the bank. He doesn't have the incentive they have here. You're going to see harder-played ball here. The other night, our right fielder Dave Coleman went against the wood for a ball, and you could hear the fence reverberate from home plate. He flew horizontally from the ground, maybe ten feet up, and he nearly got it. It was only a foul ball. You won't see that in the major leagues."

Coleman's élan is understandable, as is the enthusiasm of all of his teammates. Being in the elite Boston-farm system, they are following tough acts, and must prove themselves daily. Such players as Jim Rice and Fred Lynn played at Pawtucket before them, and the Red Sox have built their recent powerhouses mainly on farm talent. For instance, in 1978 eight of Boston's regulars had come through the system, and five had stopped off at Pawtucket. Front office people, too, are groomed in the minors as well. Darrell Johnson managed at Pawtucket before leading Boston to a pennant in 1975, and Don Zimmer, the current Boston manager, also came up through the Boston system, widely recognized as one of the best in baseball.

"Players hate to leave this organization," says Mondor. "It breaks their hearts when they're traded. It's kind of a family feeling. Just recently, I got letters from Mike Paxton, Ted Cox, and Bo Diaz. They've been traded to Cleveland, but they still write to wish everyone well. Last year, when we had an important series with Tidewater at the end of the year, some of the Boston players came down when they had a day off to cheer these guys on. That's great. I don't think you'll see that anyplace else."

The familial atmosphere has long been a Boston trademark. Tom Yawkey, the likeable and legendary Boston owner, fostered the spirit and others—such as Haywood Sullivan and current farm director Ed Kenney—have carried it on. It is a general policy of the Boston front office to repay loyalty; thus many former players, such as longtime Red Sox minor leaguer Tony Torchia who manages Bristol, remain within the system. The Red Sox, too, spare no expense getting quality people in strategic positions, such as teachers and scouts. Ted Williams, for one, is a batting instructor, and onetime Dodger star Johnny Podres is a pitching coach for Boston's minor league teams. "When I was a kid," says Mondor, "the New York Yankees had the class organization in the minors. Now, it's the Red Sox."

Not everyone is content in The System, of course. There are players who look up at the Boston team and see no hope for themselves because of the exquisite lineup. Some, such as Jack Baker, sized up an outfield that included Rice, Lynn, Dwight Evans, and Carl Yastrzemski, and decided that he wanted out. The Red Sox traded him to Cleveland for Gary Hancock. Dave Coleman, for another, said near the end of the 1978 season that he would not report to Pawtucket for another year of Triple-A ball. The twenty-seven year old was tired of waiting for his big chance.

But, for the most part, the big league talent of the Red Sox serves as an incentive, rather than a deterrent, it seems.

"It's got to do something to these kids," says Mondor, "knowing that they're walking in the footprints of giants. Take Gary Allenson, our catcher. He's behind home plate in the very spot where Carlton Fisk stood. It's a hell of a thing. You take a poor kid playing third base here—he's right at the spot following Butch Hobson."

Allenson, by the way, is one of those whom Pawtucket Manager Joe Morgan tickets for big-league stardom. A muscular, 5-foot-11, 185-pound Californian who signed out of Arizona State, Allenson made the big jump from Class A ball at Winter Haven, Fla., to Triple-A in 1978 and landed on his feet. Allenson was a club leader in every respect, batting at .300 most of the year and serving as a bulwark behind home plate with a penchant for picking off runners. His arm was recognized as one of the best in the minors.

Another player whom Morgan admires is Glenn Hoffman, a slim, 6-foot-1 shortstop who throws hard and accurately and often makes spectacular plays with his exceptional reflexes. But the manager sees him as a longer-range prospect than Allenson. He, too, came to Pawtucket in 1978 from Winter Haven, but didn't adjust as well to the higher caliber of pitching.

"Hoffman's way over his head with the bat here," Morgan says, "but he's the winning type. If he can build himself up physically, he'll be a better hitter. He doesn't run good, but he gets off the dime quickly."

It could be pitching, though, more than anything else that may be the pride of the Boston farm system these days. It is a change of pace, of course, since the Red Sox historically have recruited a plethora of powerful right-handed hitters to fit in with their friendly left field wall at Fenway Park.

"This Joel Finch is a real prospect," notes Morgan. "Chuck Rainey, too. And Burke Sutur and the kid from Holland, Win Remmerswaal. We've got a short reliever in the bullpen, Mike Burns, a lefty. He's got a big league arm, but control trouble. If he ever learns to throw strikes, he'll make it."

Bob Sprowl, another left-hander with a major league arm, was called up to Boston as the Red Sox made their September run for the pennant in 1978. Another top pitcher in the Red Sox farm system that season was Steve Schneck, a classy right-hander at Bristol of the Class AA Eastern League.

Ironically, Morgan had given up on another pitching prospect who eventually made it. But later he had to admit his mistake when Jim Wright was promoted to Boston in the summer of 1978 and did a good job for the Red Sox.

"I can't believe he's pitching that well for Boston," Morgan says. "He got killed here for two years. Last year I didn't even start him. He came to me midway through the season and asked why I wasn't using him and I told him. I told him I'd given him two years and he hadn't done the job. But then he got another chance . . . he won ten straight, all beautiful games, too. He's pitching up there the way he did in those ten games, but I didn't think he could, not with all that hanging around they have to do before pitching turns. He was a noncomplainer, though. He always said it was his fault. Not wanting to admit your own mistakes, as most people are prone to do, is an ingredient that kills a lot of people here."

Considering the geographical structure of the International League, Pawtucket is an island unto itself, alone out there in left field while the rest of the teams are grouped in cozy clatches in the South, Midwest, and New York State. Columbus and Toledo are colleagues in Ohio; Richmond, Tidewater, and Charleston are nuzzled together in the Virginia and West Virginia area; and Syracuse and Rochester are paired in New York. However, Pawtucket's syncronization with the major league team couldn't be more perfect—as Mondor puts it, "thirty-two miles clubhouse to clubhouse." Thus, the Red Sox can call up a player and fully expect him to be ready for a game on the same day. Notes Mondor: "The Red Sox needed a left-handed swinger for one game this year and called up Gary Hancock. So Gary got into his car and an hour later, he was dressing for the game at Fenway Park. Think how fluid this makes an organization. A lot of people envy us." With Boston's second-top farm team at Bristol, Conn., also virtually within the shadow of Fenway Park, this makes for one of the coziest arrangements in baseball.

The proximity to Fenway has not hurt the Pawsox' attendance, either. "Everyone said that a Triple-A club could not survive so close to the major league team," says Mondor, "but we have certainly proven them wrong."

Because of the circumstances, the first year was not so easy for Mondor, of course. "The team's franchise had been revoked by the International League," he says. "The former owners had gotten into great financial difficulties and credibility had gone down the drain. The fans had lost faith. It was just a bad scene all over." While winning the pennant in 1977, the PawSox broke attendance records on the road. But they also set a negative record at home—the smallest attendance for a pennant-winning team in the history of the International League. Mondor expected it to take three to five years to "achieve credibility," but seems to have accomplished that in two. The accomplishment is noteworthy for a man with little background in baseball—the Canadian-born Mondor never even played on his grammar school team and was in textiles until "retirement" some five years ago.

Always a passionate disciple of baseball, however, Mondor was astute enough to surround himself with savvy, aggressive people once he got into the game. One of these has been Mike Tamburro, one of the youngest and best general managers in minor league baseball. Tamburro has already made a mark for himself as General Manager of the Year at Elmira in the New York-Penn League, and like Mondor, doesn't pay attention to clocks.

"We all have the same goal here," says Tamburro. "Hey, without it you just couldn't go as hard as you can. God only knows what is going to happen. My goal here now is to help make this franchise a winner."

Tamburro's lust for success, coupled with Mondor's cockeyed optimism, gives the PawSox a couple of heavy hitters in the lineup, all right.

4

Dreams of Glory

The number one draft choice of the New York Yankees squirts a spray of tobacco juice into a paper cup and considers the burden of his position. No sweat, he decides in so many words.

"There has been little pressure on me," says Rex Hudler. "Most of the pressure's off because they know I can do it. They know I have the tools . . . that it's just a matter of time before I can put them all together."

It is not braggadocio, merely the type of high confidence you would expect from the top draft choice in 1978 of baseball's World Champions. Hudler was lured away from a football career at Notre Dame and given a reported $100,000 to sign with the Yankees—which means that George Steinbrenner and Co. think that Hudler is as good as money in the bank.

"They tell me I can make the majors in three or four years," Hudler says, "depending on how I improve each year. The Yankees believe in success at every level."

Hudler had a good first year with the bat at Oneonta in the Class A New York-Penn League, hitting in the neighborhood of .300 all season.

"I know shortstops don't have to hit too much," he says, "but hitting is a big part of my game. The Yankees want a hitting shortstop, and I'm going to try to do that for them."

Hudler is as much concerned about his defense as he is his offense this summer day in August.

"My fielding hasn't come along like I'd like," Hudler tells you through a large chaw of tobacco. "I'd like to stay down with the ball and cover more ground, and learn the different techniques that I don't really have down pat yet . . . like playing the hitters, covering second base, where to take all the throws and the cutoffs."

The Yankees had ticketed their prize catch for winter ball in Florida to pick up such basics. Hudler knows he still has a long way to go, but isn't intimidated.

"I look at the Yankees' starting lineup and it's kind of awesome. You see those people and say to yourself, 'There's no way I'll ever get there.' But you just go through each step one at a time and pretty soon you'll be up to the capability of playing ball like they do. I'm young and I have a lot of learning to do. But the players on the New York Yankees went through the same thing that I'm going through and I figure in a matter of a few years, God willing, I'll be there. A lot of it is in your head. . . . 95 percent of it is mental."

Hudler, a seventeen year old with bright red hair and an extremely polite manner—almost every sentence is prefaced by, "Sir"—not long ago was at the crossroads of his athletic career as a senior in a California high school. The Fresno native had a tough choice to make between football and baseball before the Yankees made the choice for him with their lucrative contract offer.

"Before I signed with the Yankees," Hudler remembers, "football was the first thing for me. My dad and I would always read in the newspapers about these minor league players who were married and weren't making any money at all and we always said, no, that's not for me. As football went on, I got a scholarship to Notre Dame and I was real excited about playing football in the fall. And then right before the baseball season started, the scouts said I had a chance to be drafted at the end of the year if I had a good year. I kept that out of my head, but it seemed like toward the end of the year, everybody was coming to me, everybody was wanting to talk to me."

There was good reason that Hudler was the apple of the pro scouts' eyes—he had won the triple crown in his league and played shortstop with professional efficiency.

"I made up my mind never to second-guess myself after signing with the Yankees," Hudler says, his freckled face beaming. "I put football completely out of my mind and concentrated 100 percent on baseball."

The wonderful contract was not the only reason

that he opted for baseball.

"It's a now career . . . instant. I'm seventeen years old. I looked at my age and figured I could someday make it."

Hudler expected to "come right in and play baseball," and he did. The Yankees don't let $100,000 prospects sit on the bench. "Not many people gave me a bad time about being the number one pick," says the quick-smiling youngster. "Overall, it's been a pretty good year for me."

The toughest adjustment that Hudler had to make was playing every day, as most new professional ballplayers will tell you.

"In high school, you play two games a week and when you play every day, you get more tired, your bat gets slow. My bat was getting very heavy toward the middle of the year. I didn't get that tired fielding, just batting. I was getting callouses and blisters on my hand."

Hudler discovered something about professional pitching, too.

"The pitchers in high school didn't have as good velocity; the curve balls weren't as good as they are here, either, and I had to change my hitting style. I moved up at the plate a little bit more and concentrated on making contact with the ball."

Like Hudler, Bryan Ryder is also making the transition from high school to professional ball in the summer of 1978. But his view is from the pitching mound, not the batter's box. A strong right-hander who reminds some of a young Nolan Ryan, Ryder seemed to have adjusted nicely in his first year at Oneonta.

"The first time I came here, I might have been in awe," says the eighteen-year-old native of Shrewsbury, Mass., "but after a few starts, I knew I could compete on a professional level."

As a pitcher who has to wait four days between starts, Ryder is not troubled so much by the physical aspects of the game as he is the mental.

"It's hard to get yourself up for a game when you're not playing every day," the tall, lean youngster says. "Sometimes on the road you might have to hang around your hotel room all day, and it's rough when you're pitching that night and you have to start thinking about the game. You really have to pick yourself up."

Ryder's repertoire at present includes only one pitch—a fastball—and he knows that it alone is not enough to propel him to the major leagues.

"I definitely have to get a good second pitch," he says. "My main concern right now is to learn to throw a slider—that will help me 100 percent. My curve ball isn't that good. I throw it in the dirt. Hitters here might go after it, but as you get higher, they won't go after bad pitches as much."

A product of Shrewsbury High School, Ryder signed with the Yankee organization without hesitation. There was no special loyalty to the Boston Red Sox, despite his close proximity to the team. "A Red Sox scout told me they were interested in me, but couldn't draft me until the fourth round because they had gone into the free agent market and made commitments. They felt I'd be gone before then. I wasn't a big Red Sox fan, anyway."

Upon arrival in Oneonta, Ryder caught the usual case of homesickness. "The first three days here felt like three weeks," he says. "It was my first time away. The hardest thing to do at first was to get myself to do simple things like shopping and cleaning. My family used to do all that for me."

Further complicating matters for Ryder were a couple of inauspicious pitching performances at the start.

"In my first couple of outings, I had trouble, and I think maybe part of the reason was that I started to look ahead. Everyone was telling me that by the time I was twenty-one or twenty-two, I'd be up in the majors. And that was my problem, I started thinking about getting up too fast and forgetting about the first step. I had to settle down and do my job here first."

Later, Ryder righted himself and did the things expected of him. Yankee hierarchy figure that he can make the majors in three to four years, and the good-looking pitcher sees nothing wrong with that assessment. He isn't discouraged by the current Yankee strength.

"It's definitely easier for pitchers to move up faster," he says. "There's always arm trouble on the big club. We've had two kids who have already moved up this year."

Ted Wilborn is also looking to move up, but for him the progression has not been as fast as he would like. The summer of 1978 signals his third year in professional ball, and they have all been at the Class A level.

"It seems like I'll never get to the majors," says

Wilborn, a svelte nineteen-year-old center fielder who was the NY-P League's base-stealing champ in 1978. "All those high-salaried players on the Yankees, plus my age, it seems like such a long way off. But I'll give myself two more years."

Wilborn, a Mickey Rivers look-alike, signed with the Yankees in 1976 after playing high school ball in Sacramento, California. His baseball passion notwithstanding, it took him two years of playing in the NY-P League and Florida State League before cracking the starting lineup with the Oneonta Yankees.

"The last two years, I was sitting on the bench and I was really frustrated," Wilborn says. "I was thinking about quitting . . . thinking about going to college. But I finally told myself I would go as hard at it as I can, and when I get my chance, I'm going to take advantage of it. It finally worked out."

The transition from high school to professional ball was as easy for Wilborn as stealing second base.

"I was mentally ready for all of this," he says. "I talked to a lot of people. Rowland Office and Jerry Royster are friends of mine and they prepared me. It wasn't much of a difference for me from high school, really. The roughest part of it was not playing."

Wilborn's experience marked him as a "veteran" on the Oneonta team, which in 1978 was otherwise composed of just first-year players. He enjoyed the role, and the responsibility that went along with it.

"I give a lot of help to the guys in the outfield," he says. "I feel that's the strongest part of my game

—my defense. The coaches have told me I am a major league outfielder right now. It was just something that came natural to me, so I try to share what I know."

Wilborn's experience also gave him a certain position of autonomy on the club. And he enjoyed that, too. "The manager [Art Mazmanian] lets me play my game. He has certain expectations of me and I fulfill them, and he doesn't have to say too much."

And just what expectations does Wilborn have of himself?

"Oh, to continue hitting like I have. Keep hitting, hitting for high average, getting on base . . . stealing bases."

He flashes a grin, showing metal braces on his teeth.

"Otherwise," he says, "it's back to real estate school."

Greg Cochran drapes himself across several seats in Roosevelt Stadium and watches his Jersey Indian teammates take batting practice on a warm August day. The humidity of the afternoon, coupled with several laps around the field, had matted Cochran's modish blond hair. The mustachioed pitcher fiddles with a green-striped shoe which he has just taken off and reflects on a universal baseball truth.

"The enjoyment of the game compensates for the bad parts of it, because you enjoy it so much, especially when you're going good," the pitcher says. "It's the greatest feeling in the world to go out and throw nine innings, win or lose. Throwing nine innings, I get a big kick out of that . . . just because you know you're working hard and you're keeping your team in the ballgame."

It is precisely the reason that Cochran, at the age of twenty-four and after a full college career at Arizona State and four seasons of minor-league ball, was able to continue to stick it out on the Class AA level in 1978, hoping for his chance at big-league stardom. It is the reason that the gregarious Californian was able to live away from his loved ones for so long, and put up with the many privations of minor league life.

"It's rough," he says. "We've had a lot of guys quit. You're away from your families. You can't bring them out here, because you really don't feel safe having them in the city when you're gone on road trips. I'm getting married this winter. It's been a rough summer for me . . . I've only seen my fiancée a week out of the whole summer."

Cochran, wearing a sweat shirt and powder-blue road uniform pants the Indians use for practices, cocks his head toward the sky.

"You've got to have support from somewhere," he says. "Like, my support comes from home, from my fiancée and my parents. It's very important to have someone backing you because you're in a pretty bad situation in the minors. I'm not kidding you . . . I was ready to bag it myself. I didn't because I love the game too much. But I thought about it; it crossed my mind. For instance, I probably make as much money as anybody on this team, which isn't too good, up around $1,000 a month. I was spending my whole paycheck every two weeks to get to and from the ballpark and live in the Holiday Inn. Now, that's ridiculous! That's enough to make you want to give the whole thing up."

Cochran's dilemma was solved later in the season when he and some teammates moved into a private home.

"We ended up getting the best place in the whole city. They do our wash for us; it's furnished. We come back, our sheets are changed, the beds are made. It only costs us $12.50 a week per person. So now we're saving money. But it'll probably end up with us breaking even for the summer, because of all the money we spent in the first half."

Cochran is a typical product of the high-powered college baseball system these days. But his personal history is anything but typical. A native of Whittier, California, about thirty-five miles south of Los Angeles, Cochran played the outfield and first base most of the way through high school, "but there didn't seem to be much future in it." So he became a pitcher in his senior year, and a good one at that, judging by the Philadelphia Phillies' interest in him. He was drafted by the Phillies, but opted to go to college because his longtime dream was to play for Bobby Winkles at Arizona State. (As it turned out, he did play for Arizona State, but not for Winkles. Shortly after recruiting Cochran, the well-known college coach went to the major leagues.)

"Much to my dismay, I had a rough first three years," Cochran recalls. "I had some arm problems and I didn't know if I was going to make it. Then the Lord helped me out. It was really kind of miraculous. The minute my senior year started, it was perfect. Nothing could have gone wrong. I was 14-1; I threw 140 innings and pitched in the College World Series in Omaha before 13,000 fans. It was great, I was so jacked up."

Cochran was drafted by Oakland on the second round of the annual baseball draft and was sent to Modesto of the California League in July 1975. "My first year was pretty rough there," Cochran says. "But the next year I went back and was 9-8 and third in the league in earned-run average. It was just a matter of learning how to pitch, keeping the ball down, learning to throw strikes. Control probably was my biggest asset."

In 1977, Cochran was jumped from Class A ball to Double-A, starting the season with Chattanooga in the Southern League. Midway through June he was moved up to Triple-A, pitching for Oakland's San Jose team in the Pacific Coast League.

"That's a heck of a league," notes Cochran, now fitting his cleated shoe back on his foot. "Everything is geared for the hitters. The parks are not that big, the air is lighter, and everywhere you go—Albuquerque, Salt Lake City, San Jose—the ball travels like crazy. The lights are excellent and you seem to face all the hitters—the young kids that are on their way to the major leagues, and then the older guys who are on their way down. It was a nightmare for some pitchers. I know it was for me. Still, it was great to be up that high."

Cochran was looking forward to another season

in Triple-A ball in 1978, but baseball's Domino Principle knocked him down to Jersey City and the Double-A Eastern League.

"I thought I was going to make the Triple-A club this year, but Oakland's Vida Blue deal [involving seven players] knocked some guys down from the big club to Triple-A and consequently bumped everyone else down the line. It was really a psychological letdown for me."

Cochran reflects for a moment, smiling and shaking his head.

"But that Pacific Coast League, that's really a nice league. You feel like a ballplayer up there. You dress nice, you fly, you stay in good hotels, you're in the great cities. Hawaii is in there, which is really a fun trip. That's all part of it. There's a little bit of glamour there. You feel yourself getting closer to the big leagues . . ."

The psychological implications of a demotion at the start of a new season was further complicated by other discomforts.

"This is the worst league I've played in as far as conditions go," Cochran emphasizes. "For instance, here we have a situation of battling just to find housing. Consequently, that affected my pitching at the beginning of the year, because I didn't start out too strong. You're battling your environment a lot. The bus rides . . . the badly lit parks . . . it's rough."

Cochran also was bothered by apparent injustices in the A's organization.

"They're baby-sitting in our Triple-A club," Cochran says. "All five starting pitchers in Vancouver are twenty-one years old and below. We've got guys here that deserve to be in the rotation up there right now."

New Jersey is called the "Garden State," but Cochran found Jersey City to be less than the garden spot of the minor league circuit, and social activity was practically nil.

"There's not much to do around here," he says. "Most of the guys just spend their summers lying out in the sun, getting tans to take home with them. My biggest pastime is golf, but I can't do that because there are not too many golf courses within reasonable driving distance. And we don't have transportation, anyway. A lot of guys play backgammon, cards, read books. I think I've read the whole *New York Times* best-seller list this summer. It's cheap entertainment."

Cochran can always fall back on his degree in marketing from Arizona State should he flunk out of baseball, but that's a security blanket he hopes never to use. He has not laid out a specific timetable for making the major leagues—he will stay on the track as long as he sees himself moving forward.

"I'm planning on giving baseball a good shot," Cochran says, "because I think I can pitch in the big leagues. I really do. As long as I see myself progressing, there's no use giving up."

At this point in the season, Cochran—a stylish right-hander with excellent control—was leading the Jersey staff in complete games. As much as he was mastering opposing hitters, he was also mastering his own psyche.

"The mental aspect of pitching is the most important thing," he says. "Being a successful pitcher is having confidence and knowing you can do it. A lot of guys throw hard, but if you don't know how to pitch, have the confidence in yourself, you'll never make it. I gained a lot of confidence in my last year of college when I was successful. But still I wasn't a complete pitcher. Just now I'm starting to become the kind of pitcher I want to be. Control is a big thing . . . not walking people. I usually don't walk too many people when I pitch anymore. It's a big asset. You just throw the ball up there and let them hit it. There aren't too many .300 hitters around anymore and you're not going to get knocked out every time you pitch while throwing strikes. Throwing your breaking ball when you're behind is a big asset for a pitcher, too. I've got confidence enough to do that now. It's really just going out there and believing in yourself—believing that you're better than the guy at the plate. But you have to go out and work hard every day; you have to bust your butt to make it. Otherwise, it's not going to work out."

Cochran doesn't mind "busting his butt," either, before the usual small audiences they get at Roosevelt Stadium.

"Oh, sure, it's great to have people cheering for you all the time and seeing a lot of faces," he says, "but you're a virtual unknown in the minors anyway —so that doesn't bother me. We had ninety-two people here the other night and I threw one of my better games. It doesn't matter to me one way or the other. I'm just out there trying to do the best I can."

* * *

"When you get to the higher levels of minor league ball, you find players with different attitudes. They are hardened by four or five years of experience—and built-up frustrations."

That recent assessment by a minor league coach might be particularly relevant to the World Champion New York Yankee farm system these days. They seem to lead the minors in frustrations—at least at West Haven.

"Let's look at it realistically," says shortstop Dennis Sherrill. "The Yankees are loaded with talent, and they aren't going to make a lot of changes by bringing up players from the minor leagues. I think just about everyone in the Yankee minor league system would like to be traded."

Sherrill's feelings seem to be representative of many Yankee minor league players, especially on the Double-A and Triple-A levels, who believe they have no place to go in the organization but out.

Sherrill uses the example of outfielder Willie Upshaw, who was drafted by Toronto and wound up becoming the Blue Jays' regular left fielder.

"If he were still in the Yankee chain, he'd be in Tacoma [Triple-A Pacific Coast League], or even here at West Haven," says Sherrill. "But he got a good break, and that's what a lot of guys around here are looking for. There's not much chance of making it with the Yankees, not with all the talent they have."

Once a top draft choice of the Yankees, the twenty-two-year-old Sherrill was back in 1978 after sitting out a season. He was disappointed by his demotion in 1977 from Syracuse (Triple-A) to Fort Lauderdale (Single-A) and "retired" for one year.

Sherrill was among many good prospects in 1978 at West Haven, a hard-hitting team with a predominately left-handed lineup that would fit in nicely with the cozy right field wall at Yankee Stadium. Other players with potential included outfielders Rick Stenholm and Buck Showalter, first baseman Jim McDonald, second baseman Roger Holt, catcher Mike Heath (who had a cup of coffee in New York in 1978 before the big club traded him to the Texas Rangers), outfielder-third baseman Joe Lefebvre and pitchers Paul Semall and Chris Welsh.

"Lefebvre [La-FAY] is the kind of guy who'll catch your eye because he's a scrambler," said West Haven Manager Stump Merrill. "He got off to a slow start, but he's hitting well lately. We play him at third base to get more punch in the lineup, but basically he's an outfielder. The Yankees thought about making him into a catcher this spring because he has such a good arm."

Merrill also is high on Semall, a 6-foot-4, 200-pound right-hander.

"He's very poised for a young man just a year out of college," the manager says of the Ohio State product.

The boxes at Quigley Stadium are named after former West Haven players in the majors. Not surprisingly, only one, Ron Guidry, is currently a New York Yankee among the boxes named for active players. And the trade in 1978 of Mickey Klutts and Dell Alston to the Oakland A's provided two more former West Haveners that now play for other organizations.

Merrill, however, does not necessarily see this as a pattern of the future. His view of the Yankee organization obviously does not coincide with his players' opinions.

"There's a lot of talk about where you can go in this organization," says the West Haven manager. "But guys think if the Yankees can't use you, someone else can. I personally think the Yankees will depend more on the farm system now that they've built it up. For awhile there, they had to go out and get veteran players because their own farmhands weren't ready."

Most baseball players don't choose to make a career out of the minors, but for Tom Farrias it's starting to feel that way. The summer of 1978 is his sixth season in professional ball and he has hit every rung on the ladder but the top one. He is starting to feel pessimistic about his chances of making the major leagues.

"As long as I have a uniform on, I have a shot to make it," says Farrias, then adds with a half-hearted smile: "But realistically, looking at our system and what's happened to me, I don't believe I'll make it in the Red Sox organization in the big leagues . . ."

The smooth-throwing right-hander has cause to worry, although he is the ace relief pitcher for the Bristol Red Sox in the Double-A Eastern League. He is twenty-seven years old, for one thing. For another, the parent team is loaded with talent and multi-year contracts.

"Being in Boston's minor league system is kind of frustrating because they're pretty well set up there now," says Farrias. "There's not much you can do. We have a lot of people in our minor league organization I feel can be in the big leagues for quite a few other teams. You can have a real good year and still not be promoted in the Boston system. It works on your mind all the time. Boston has to be one of the toughest organizations to make it in."

Aside from the talent on top, there is another reason why players perhaps find the Boston system so tough in which to rise. The Red Sox traditionally refuse to rush players through their minor league development, seeking success at every level. Farrias has certainly found this to be true in his case. The native of New Bedford, Mass., took the normally structured route through the Boston system with stops at Class A ball in Winter Haven (Fla.), Double-A at Bristol, and Triple-A at Pawtucket. But after a couple of years with the International League team, just one step below the majors, Farrias was dropped back to Bristol.

That had to be the most disappointing blow of his career, but it didn't knock Farrias completely out of the box.

"It's easy to get down on yourself in this game," says Farrias, a young man with curly black hair, a strong face, and piercing eyes. "But if you keep doing that, you find yourself carrying a lunch pail the next spring. It's people who can get out of the depressions quicker who are a lot better off in this game. I think my experience has helped me in this regard. I was never like this three or four years ago. If I went out and had a bad game, I really took it hard. You have a bad temper when you first come up, but that's something you have to work on. If you let the game go to your head, it really messes you up, and it can mess up your life as well. In the whole realm of things, baseball is really nothing. It's a game, that's all. And if you start thinking that way, playing hard and doing the best you can, then nothing will bother you."

Farrias's maturity is a steadying influence on the young Bristol staff. Because of his age and experience, he has slid easily into the role of pitching guru.

"What I'm looking for right now is getting into the coaching aspect of this organization," says Farrias. "I like it very much—it's what I'd like to do for as long as I can do it. But until that role comes, though, you never get your thoughts out of making the big leagues. I'm still thinking I can make the majors. As long as I feel that way, I think I'll produce on the field. Realistically, I'm at an age now that if I don't make it this year, then I am not going to make it. But right now I have the role of the ace of the bullpen, I believe, and I come into games in a lot of key situations. And if I don't believe I can make it to the big leagues, I'm just going to go out and throw the ball and not help the club, and I'm not going to help myself and I might as well not play."

Steve Schneck is another right-hander on the

Bristol club, but not *just* another right-hander. Just turned twenty-two, the tall, slim pitcher is among the prize prospects in the Red Sox organization and seems headed for major league stardom. Schneck was signed out of a junior college in Michigan in 1976 and showed immediate results.

The pleasant, blond youngster says he is enjoying the minor leagues so far, and well he should. Schneck has shown solid progress at every stop he's made in the Boston chain—at Elmira in the New York-Penn League, Winter Haven in the Florida State League, and at Bristol, where he became the ace of the staff in 1978.

Holding his own competitively at every level so far, Schneck's confidence is quickly matching his pitching performances.

"When I was first signed, I was sent to an extended spring training in St. Petersburg, Fla., and learned a lot down there under Eddie Papowski," says Schneck. "That's helped me considerably. I learned to concentrate on the batters more and bear down . . . not give in to a hitter. You have to say to yourself, 'I'm better than this hitter.' That is the attitude I'm taking right now, and it's working."

Schneck's personal timetable is developing just as he expected it would.

"When I first signed, my goal was to take one step at a time, and try not to stay two years with one team, and that's the way it's been so far. Next year, I'm almost 100 percent sure I'll be at Pawtucket. I'm going to go into spring training with the frame of mind that I *will* make the team, because I figure the

Red Sox will have to protect me after the season I've had here. [At the time of the interview, Schneck had just won his sixteenth game and was heading for a Bristol club record.] So I figure I'll be at Pawtucket in 1979 and by 1980, I should be in Boston. I'll only be twenty-four by that time and will still have a long time ahead of me for a major league career."

Schneck isn't complacent enough, though, to think that he can make the big leagues merely by tossing his glove on the mound.

"I have to throw my fastball across more consistently," he says amid the horseplay of the Bristol dugout.

As bats and expletives drop, Schneck explains quietly:

"In the past, I haven't had any problems with my fastball. But this year I've been inconsistent throwing it for strikes. I'd say I hit the strike zone with it about 50 to 75 percent of the time. It should be better than that, really. I've had good control with my slider so far. I've had so much confidence in that pitch—going for strikes on 3-2 and 2-2 counts—and I'll come back to that every time I need to. But I need more than that one pitch to make it."

As confident as he is, Schneck is somewhat intimidated by the talent in front of him.

"That always enters your mind," says Schneck. "You're always looking at the Boston club—you know, how young the players are. And the Red Sox have a lot of young players on their pitching staff . . . Dennis Eckersley, and a lot of players that have a lot of years ahead of them. This year, it was hard on a lot of ballplayers in our organization because we were just so backed up with so many good players, especially pitching, that some of them who were in Triple-A had to be dropped all the way down to Single-A.''

Mike O'Berry is aware of all that Red Sox talent on top, too. As a catcher, he is playing a waiting game behind the likes of Carlton Fisk, among others.

"It doesn't really scare you, because to stay in this organization I figure you have to have some talent," says O'Berry, a soft-spoken, broad-shouldered young man. "But it can be disheartening to know that even if you have a good year at one place, you'll probably be back at the same place the next year because of all the talent they have in this organization. But you really can't give up, because you always have the chance of being picked up by somebody else."

The 1978 season was the second one at Bristol for O'Berry, one of the better defensive catchers in the minor leagues in 1978. A product of South Alabama under former major leaguer Eddie Stanky. O'Berry played at Winter Haven and Winston-Salem in the two seasons prior to joining the Bristol Red Sox in 1977. He was expected to move up to Pawtucket for the 1978 season, but was passed over for a younger prospect from Class A ball, Gary Allenson.

"This is not a game to play if you just want to play it," O'Berry says, "because the money's not that good in the minor leagues. You really have to want to make it and dedicate yourself and have the desire, especially to put up with the conditions of minor league ball. Everybody knows how it's going to be once you make the majors, so it gives you incentive."

O'Berry keeps talking through playful kibitzing by teammates who are now out of the locker room in abundance. One screams over, "Bullshit!" as O'Berry makes a point; another drops some bats on purpose. O'Berry smiles.

"I've gone back to school and gotten my degree, so there's no problem. I don't have a timetable set. I'm just twenty-four now and in the next couple of years I'll have some idea of where I'm going because I've had a fairly good year this year. Next year, if I have a good year and nothing happens, the writing's kind of on the wall. But if I didn't think I could make it, I'd get out right now. I think I have a chance and people in the organization think I have a chance. So, therefore, I'll give it my best and hope my chance will come. It might be next year; it might be in three years. There are a lot of twenty-seven and twenty-eight-year-old rookies in the major leagues and if you get there at that age, there's still enough time for a pretty good pension."

Meanwhile, O'Berry must put up with the often exasperating conditions of minor league life. It's a test of endurance for him.

"The worst part for me," he says, "are the playing conditions, especially the bad lighting. If you go to some parks—like in this league, Jersey City—the lighting is so bad you can't really see. Other places you go, the lights may be all right but then you have street lights in the background and it makes it tough on hitting."

O'Berry abhors the living conditions as well. ("You come into a small town like this, and it's hard to find a place to stay because people won't give you a break on the lease. We go three, four weeks into a season before we find someplace permanent.") Nor is he too thrilled about the anonymity. ("You can have a great game and nobody knows about it.") But at least in Bristol, fan support is a lot better than, say, at Jersey City.

O'Berry chuckles, recalling a story in this regard.

"We were just playing Jersey City and I was talking to one of the players there. He went down with some teammates to a local mall to sign autographs and people in the city were asking them what they were doing in Jersey City. They'd been there five months and people didn't know they had a team there!"

Game time is several hours away and Buddy Hunter is out checking the weather and the field. He is fully dressed in his home whites, always a step ahead of his teammates on the Pawtucket Red Sox. As team captain and player-coach, he has to set an example.

"I think we'll be able to get this one in," Hunter says, holding his hand out as a fine mist sprays McCoy Stadium.

The veteran second baseman has played in worse weather, he acknowledges. He is long acquainted with the erratic New England summers, and other inconsistent areas. Over the long seasons of playing the minor league circuit, he has seen a lot.

"I've been playing minor league ball for ten years, and that's quite a feat, I guess," he says. "If you don't have a good year after good year in this business, they just forget you."

Except for playing in twenty-two major league games in three different summers with the Boston Red Sox, Hunter has been a captive of the minor leagues for his entire career. And unless something drastic happens in Boston, Hunter figures to close out his playing career in the minors. He is nearing his thirty-second birthday, an "old man" for an athlete.

"My future's going to lie in managing," he says firmly, "and I'm going to set my goals high. I didn't quite set them high enough as a player, but I'm going to set them high as a manager. I want to manage in the big leagues. And I'm off to a good start. There aren't many thirty-one-year-old men who are thinking about managing in the big leagues."

In this regard, Hunter is off on the right foot as a player-coach on the Pawtucket team—a dual position he has warmly embraced for three summers.

"It's sort of my job to answer any questions that the younger players have, on the field or off the field," Hunter explains. "I enjoy helping the younger players out. It gives me great satisfaction, for instance, to tell a young kid like a Glenn Hoffman [the Pawtucket shortstop] that he's doing something wrong, and having the kid go out there and work on it and try to improve himself. And then when I see that he actually does improve it in a game, why, it's a great feeling."

Though ten years have passed, it wasn't too long ago in Hunter's mind that he was in Glenn Hoffman's position—a strong, young player with major league stars in his eyes and a world of potential. A native of Omaha, Nebraska, Hunter was drafted by the Red Sox out of Pershing College in 1969 and moved right into the pretigious Eastern League at Pittsfield. He remained at the Double-A level for two years before his promotion to Boston's International League team at Louisville and has remained at the Triple-A level ever since.

"I grew up in a baseball family, so it's in my blood," says Hunter, explaining his tenacious hold on baseball despite the disappointment of failing to make the majors. "My uncle played ten years with the Dodgers, and I had two cousins play with the Dodgers also. My father signed a pro baseball contract, too, and I lived next to a baseball park when I grew up as a kid in Omaha. My wife always said that baseball is my first love and is even now, more than her. I kind of disagree with her there, but I do love baseball. It's still in my system."

Hunter's intense passion for the sport has helped alleviate some of the pain of minor league life for him and his family.

"It's probably been rougher on my wife than me," he says. "The only rough part for me is going down to spring training and spending the first month of the season up here in Pawtucket without my family.

I have an older boy who's in school now and they have to stay back until the completion of the term. So I'm away from my family for about two and a half months, which is really hard. My wife has the bulk of the problems. She has to get the packing done, and she has to move the family around. It's a tough life for her ... but I have a very understanding wife who loves the game."

There are compensations for Lori Hunter, though.

"She likes to travel and meet different people, and we've made a lot of interesting friends through baseball," explains her husband. "It makes up for the hardships."

Hunter's even temperament has helped him ride out the psychological storms of minor league living.

"It can be quite depressing," he says, "to go out and play for a few hundred fans, especially after you've been in Triple-A ball as long as I have. It's tough to get up for a game. But, you know, I don't even think about that anymore. I guess I don't think of minor league life as a very big struggle. I'm sure there are a lot of people out there right now who would give their right arm to be where I am."

It isn't all glamour, though—especially the road trips. Says Hunter: "You can't play baseball and do as much traveling as we do and stay out all night having a good time. There's not enough time for that. I try to get as much sleep as I can on road trips. I usually can't get to sleep until 1:30 or 2 o'clock in the morning after games, and I like to get about eight hours. And when you wake up at ten or eleven, you only have a few hours before you have to get on the bus for the park. Batting practice starts at five o'clock, usually. So you don't have that much time really to get on the town."

Hunter's existence on the road can be as mundane as any traveling salesman's.

"I like to stay in my hotel room and watch soap operas. I know that quite a few players watch them. It's kind of relaxing. Instead of walking around town during the day and knocking yourself out, you sort of lie back in your bed and relax. It's kind of peaceful. I might also write letters home, or grab a bite to eat before I have to go out to the ballpark."

In Pawtucket, Hunter plays his baseball in front of "the best and most knowledgeable fans in the nation. New England fans know their baseball. It's great to see a fan argue, have something to say. A lot of parks you go into, fans don't have much to say . . . they don't root. Here, if you make a mistake people will boo you, and they have a right to do that. You pay a couple of dollars to get in, you ought to get your money's worth."

Especially pleasing to Hunter has been his work under the redoubtable Joe Morgan, a classic baseball man who has won a couple of Manager of the Year titles in the minors. Not only has Hunter learned about baseball from the Pawtucket manager, but about the human condition.

"Joe has told me that managing in the minors is a very lonely job," says Hunter. "You can't really associate with the players that much. And there isn't the press that follows you around like in the majors, or sportswriters that you can hang around with. You always are by yourself. You get more time to think about the games that way. I think it's a great teaching tool to be by yourself and think about the game. But you really have no one to communicate with, and that's the toughest part of the job. I'm sure I'll struggle as a manager, if I do get a job after playing."

Terry Ordway is one of the many who never made it to the major leagues. But he certainly had fun trying.

"Like almost every American boy," he says, "I grew up playing baseball. And for me to be offered a professional contract was probably the most unbelievable thing that I could ever have imagined, because somebody was actually going to pay me to do something that I enjoyed."

Ordway shakes his head. "The best way for me to compare this was to look at some of my buddies back home, the ones that are the fishing and hunting nuts. They would say, 'What's it like?' And I would say, 'What would you do right now if a man walked in here and offered you a few thousand dollars bonus, and gave you $500 a month to do nothing but fish for the rest of the summer?' Of course, most of them would fall off their barstools if they tried to imagine that!"

Ordway pitched in the New York Yankee farm system, mostly at the Double-A level, for four years, from 1967–1970. The Thurman Munsons and Ron Blombergs passed him by, and Ordway eventually wound up as a coach in a public school system in Maine. In 1978, he became a professional again—as a pitching coach with the Yankees' Class A farm team in Oneonta. Not far removed from youthful dreams, Ordway has no problem identifying with the Oneonta hopefuls.

"As it was for me," he says, "it must be unbelievable for these kids, too. Probably most of them would be here for less money a month, and no meal money. Mentally, they might suffer a lot. And sure, there are all types of frustrations and physical hardships. But I go back to the avid fisherman who walks twenty miles to his secluded little pond, the hardship with the insects, sleeping on the rocks . . . really, it's almost the same thing."

Ordway is part of a coaching staff of four at Oneonta (including Manager Art Mazmanian)—an unheard-of teaching complement on the minor league level. But, apparently, it is becoming typical in the Yankee system under hard-driving Jack Butterfield, the new director of minor league operations.

"As long as Jack can do what he wants to do as far as development of players," says Ordway, "there's no question in my mind that the Yankee farm system will be the best in baseball. He has organized the minor leagues so that each team has a manager and at least two coaches. Another specializes in pitching throughout the system. It's a very logical thing to do. If you pay hundreds of thousands of dollars for an eighteen-year-old talent, then shuffle him off to a team that can't give him any attention, it's money thrown out. This system today is a lot different than when I played ten years ago. I only played four years, but I had six or seven different managers and no coaches. Nobody stayed around long enough to teach us anything."

That obviously is not the case in 1978 at Oneonta.

"This is very close to college ball in that the players still have that rah-rah collegiate type of attitude and a sharp desire to learn," notes Ordway. "This is the first pro experience for these kids. They don't even complain about the long bus rides. It's all new and wonderful to them."

Ordway himself was a college player at both the University of Arizona and the University of Maine at Orono before his professional career was cut short by, among other things, his propensity for gopher balls.

He grins, recalling one such lusty shot off him. "I was pitching for Binghamton against Pittsfield in the Eastern League. Well, there was a stream that ran behind the park and atmospheric conditions were such that the fog was unbelievable. You could hardly see anything, and I threw a nice pitch to Tony Conigliaro's younger brother, Billy, and he hit a ball that from my standpoint was going to be a home run. It went up into the smog and fog. I turned around and looked and Bobby Cantrell, our center fielder, had turned his back to home plate and run all the way to the wall, turned around and faced the infield, and hit his glove once as if he were going to catch it.

"He put his glove up for about ten seconds and

then in frustration dropped both his hands to his side. And that was it. The ball disappeared. So my heart went from home run, to, boy, I'm lucky, he's going to catch it, to, where the hell did the ball go? After the inning was over, I went into the dugout. Of course the umpire had called it a home run. I said, 'Bobby, what happened?' He said, 'I didn't know where it was going. I couldn't see it, I didn't have any idea where it was. But I did hear it hit way out in the woods somewhere.' I never forgave him for that."

5

On the Road

The bus rumbled up the highway while Dan Argee juggled two hamburgers and a soda in his lap. He had had more than his share of bus rides in the minor leagues, he said.

"In the Southern League, we used to travel at night," the veteran first baseman recollected. "We'd finish a game and then travel to our next city. We'd get in maybe three or four in the morning, but then we could sleep all day. And riding at night, there's usually not much traffic, and all you can do really is sleep."

This was a road trip on a Sunday in June of 1978 —the Jersey Indians on their way to Connecticut for a game with the West Haven Yankees. It had become a classic scene, the two-hour trip nearly doubled by a traffic tie-up on Route 95 north. At one point, the bus driver read twenty-three pages of

Return to Eden without the vehicle moving 100 yards. The players who had fallen asleep on the trip when the bus was moving were awakened by the lack of motion. When traffic picked up, many of them went back to sleep.

Argee was one of those awake, sharing a Burger King dining experience with teammates Leroy Robbins, a third baseman, and Mack Harrison, a shortstop. The twenty-five-year-old Argee was a four-year veteran of the Oakland A's organization who spent the 1978 season shuttling between the Jersey Indians of the Eastern League and Charlotte of the Southern League, where he was optioned on loan to the Baltimore Orioles organization. At one point in his career, he felt that he had taken one bus ride too many with the Indians, and decided to go home to Sacramento, California.

"I really didn't think I would come back," he said. "And if I had found a good job while I was home, I probably wouldn't be here right now."

He started on his second Whopper, and continued his story.

"I was having a great time, water-skiing and everything. But then I realized I missed it, I missed the game, I missed the guys. And there was this car payment, too. I came back with one purpose—to hit .300. I wanted to prove that to myself and everyone, that I could hit .300."

The Jersey Indian players had gathered at Roosevelt Stadium in Jersey City for the eleven a.m. trip, struggling onto the bus after a night game at home. They expected to arrive in West Haven at one

p. m., but it took them more time to drive to Connecticut than it usually took the New York Mets to fly to St. Louis. The Indians finally rolled into New Haven at 2:45 p.m., and trainer Walter Horn announced, "Bus to the stadium leaves at 3:30." This did not give the Jersey players much time to eat before the game. There was a typical minor league snafu to boot. The hotel accommodations had been somehow bollixed. Horn, who also acted as the unofficial traveling secretary for the Indians, led them into their supposed hotel, then quickly led them out again.

"Something's fouled up," he said. "I'm not sure if we're staying here."

"That's what we get for playing for Jersey City!" shouted one player, inserting an expletive before Jersey City.

After reloading the luggage, the Indians used the delay to look for restaurants suitable to their $7.50-per-day meal allowance. There was a rush for the local Burger King. Nearly forty-five minutes later, Horn announced that the hotel would in fact accept the team. The time was now 3:25.

"The bus won't leave until 4:30," he said.

That meant no batting practice for the last-place Indians, who were to meet the first-place West Haven Yankees in a twi-night doubleheader. But the Jersey players instead took their batting practice against the Yankees with a fourteen-hit attack in the first game that resulted in a 15–0 rout. Ray Cosey drove in eight runs for the Indians with three hits, including a grand-slam homer. The second game also went to the Indians, 4–3, ending the stormy day with a rainbow. "It's about time we had a little fun," said Jersey Manager John Kennedy. "You can only have fun when you're winning."

Mike Norris had as much fun winning as anyone else on the Indians, but this particular night he was more concerned about his future in baseball. Once considered a prize pitching prospect by Charles O. Finley, Norris had developed arm problems while with the A's and was sent down to the minors to work things out. Now he had become disillusioned with the Oakland owner and hoped to be traded out of the organization. "If you hear of anything about a trade, give me a call in my room no matter the time," he told everyone after the bus returned to the hotel around midnight. The June 15 deadline having passed, Norris readjusted his thinking the next day, when he was scheduled to pitch the third game of the series against the angered Yankees. "The whole thing has made me stronger," he said. "About twenty minutes to three in the morning, when I knew I wasn't going to be traded, suddenly I got stronger."

Norris didn't look that strong that night on the mound, but managed to struggle to a 6–2 victory, working eight innings, throwing 147 pitches, and issuing six walks. He was halfway pleased with his performance. "My delivery still is a little off," he said. "The next start, maybe I'll be better. And pretty soon I'll put it all together again."

He sighed.

"Six walks, you can't pitch up there with six walks."

"Up there" was the majors, where they didn't have to take arduous bus rides.

"Makes me remember Mrs. Fridley's fourth-grade field trips," cracked one Jersey player as he boarded a yellow school bus for the ride back to the hotel.

A handful of players who had saved up their meal-money allowances decided to splurge and go to a Chinese restaurant. It was late, said one player, "but maybe we can talk the guy into letting us eat." Most of the players went to sleep.

The next day, Argee's grand-slam homer in the ninth inning earned the Indians a 7–3 victory and a four-game sweep of the Yankees, a team that had embarrassed them several times earlier in the season. That earned a special treat for the Indians on the way to their next stop. En route to Reading, Pa., Kennedy ordered the bus driver to pull into a McDonald's so the players could get a late-night snack. It was about 11:40 p.m. when the bus finally hit the highway for the four-hour trip to the Pennsylvania city and Kennedy could settle back and reflect on his personal dreams.

"I'm here for only one reason and that's to make it back to the major leagues again as a coach or manager," said Kennedy, a well-traveled utility infielder who played for the Los Angeles Dodgers, among other teams. "I'm not going to manage in the minor leagues forever. I can't afford it, financially. I have a family to support back in Boston. Meanwhile, I'm living in a motel and eating out every night."

This was Kennedy's fourth year as a minor league manager, his third season in the Class AA Eastern League. He previously managed for Boston's Bristol franchise, but an argument with management resulted in his dismissal.

The bus rocked softly as it sped through the Lehigh Valley and soon it was pulling up to the Abraham Lincoln Motor Inn, the Indians' place in Reading that boasted a bona fide slice of Americana: John Philip Sousa, the great orchestra leader, supposedly died there. But all the Indians were concerned about at this point was a comfortable bed. It was 3:30 in the morning and in 10½ hours, the Jersey players were scheduled to face the Reading Phillies, another of the Eastern League's tougher teams.

Once again, the checking-in process was delayed by some trouble.

"No keys until this phone bill is paid," said the clerk behind the desk, producing a list of allegedly unpaid calls from the Indians' last visit to the Abe Lincoln. The players began to sack out on couches in the lobby, softly cursing the Eastern League and the Jersey Indians. Finally, Kennedy convinced the desk clerk to give the players their keys.

"But there won't be any phones in your rooms," the clerk warned.

It was four a. m. by the time the players got to their rooms. The bus taking them to the park for an afternoon doubleheader was to depart at 12:15.

"Better leave a wake-up call," said one player to his roommate.

"It'll be tough without a phone," the roommate replied.

Somehow, the Jersey Indians managed to get to the park in time. Later, they wished they hadn't—after dropping both halves of the doubleheader, 10–9 and 3–1. In the opener, Jersey relievers failed to hold a 9–7 lead late in the game. In the second game, Reading southpaw Jeff Schneider stifled the Indian bats. Afterward, Jersey players sought their first good meal on this five-day trip, some winding up at an Italian restaurant.

"I'll bet there are some guys here who won't have one decent meal on this whole trip," Kennedy was saying. "Sure, $7.50 a day isn't a lot of money to eat on, but sometimes they'd rather spend it on a couple of beers than a good meal."

The meal-allowance figure is only reflective of the general minor league salary scale. In 1978, the pay scale on the Jersey team ranged from $600 to $2,000 a month a player, the average somewhere in the $800 range.

"I've got $50 to my name," said one Indian. "I had to write home for money to buy a couple of shirts. I'm making $600 a month and that's just not enough."

Another of the lesser-paid Indians, Leroy Robbins, noted: "I'll be lucky if I break even this summer. My wife and I both worked during the off-season, but now she's here and not working. I really don't want to dip into our savings, but trying to live in the Jersey City area on a minor league salary is tough, very tough."

However, all of the privations of minor league life are quickly forgotten in the euphoria of playing winning baseball, which the Indians managed to do on the last day of this successful road trip. They finished with a flair, sweeping a doubleheader from Reading as Greg Cochran pitched an 11–0 shutout in the first game and Dennis Haines drove in the winning runs with a two-out double in the 8–7 nightcap. That gave the Indians six victories in eight games on this road swing against two of three teams battling for the first-half EL pennant.

"There's such a difference around here when we're winning," said Robbins. "When we're losing, all of those problems we have off the field are magnified. When we're winning, we can forget all about them. It's amazing what a little success can do for an athlete."

The players then stocked up at Burger King for the 2½-hour ride home. This trip was going to be fun.

Mornings are no time for sleeping on road trips, even after a late night game. This day, under a glaring sun, the fatigued Bellingham Mariners are holding a ten a. m. workout. Two pitchers, two catchers, and the team's entire complement of outfielders are present. The scene takes place on the Chemeketa Community College baseball field in Salem, Ore., home of the Salem Senators.

"What you've got to develop is some pride," Manager Bob Didier is telling his players.

Every young face pays serious attention.

"You've got to work on your communication, helping one another out, and everytime you throw the ball you've got to have a purpose behind it."

Didier pauses for effect.

"Communicate, work hard, have a purpose in whatever you do," he emphasizes, then sends his players out on the field.

This is a commonplace scene on the Class A level of baseball, about as low as you can get in professional ball. The lowest are the rookie leagues. The six-to-eight-hour road trips on an archaic bus dubbed the "Yellow Banana," followed by a night game and then a morning practice seem to be about par for the course. The night before, the Mariners had lost a Northwest League game to the Salem team, and Didier was not especially happy.

"If you're not going to be aggressive and hard-nosed, just get the hell out of here," he told his players. "We're a disgrace to the Seattle Mariners to lose to this team."

On this sun-kissed morning, Didier works especially hard with Jorge Acosta, a sixteen-year-old Puerto Rican. Didier discovered early in the season that Acosta did not have the quickness to play the infield, so he is trying to convert him into a catcher. The player's inability to speak English got him into trouble the night before when a Salem batter bunted in front of home plate. Because Acosta didn't know how to say, "I got it," there had been a mix-up and the man reached base safely.

Now Didier, and his coaching assistant, Jack Pryor, are teaching the basics, leaving absolutely nothing to the imagination. The simple act of catching a ball and throwing it back to the infield is broken down into several basic steps. Acosta listens carefully.

It is light years away from the Kingdome, where the parent Seattle Mariners play, but every man out of the twenty-eight on that Oregon road trip believes he can make the big leagues.

"If he doesn't," says Didier, "he doesn't belong here."

Dave Valle is one of those trying. Earlier in the season, he was playing for his high school team in the Queens section of New York City, about ten minutes from midtown Manhattan. A catcher, Valle was taken in the second round of the June free agent draft by the Mariners and given a bonus guessed to be in the neighborhood of $30,000. Valle was guaranteed money for future education, should he want to go to college, and he was sent 3,000 miles to Bellingham, Washington, to play baseball for $500 a month.

Valle was a .550 hitter in his senior year in high school and thought that was pretty good—until he found that everyone else on the Bellingham team had hit .500 in high school and was an all-stater. In his first professional game, Valle collected three hits and thought, "Just like high school." But then the hits became less frequent as he discovered that pitchers threw with more velocity and greater variety in the pros. Valle's batting average dropped, and so did his confidence.

"The hard thing is not the physical, but the mental," says the seventeen-year-old Valle.

If not for a tight friendship with Mike Moore, a second-year first baseman from Yakima, Valle might have been gone long before the season was over. Moore knew how to bounce back from an 0-for-4 game.

"Mike's helped me a lot," Valle says. "When I'm down, he gets me up."

Valle gave himself five years to make the major leagues.

Like Valle, many of the players did not have spring training, but came directly to the Mariners from high school or college after being drafted in June. Thus, their "spring training" takes place during the summer.

It is a struggle, to be sure. Ill-lit parks and wild pitchers make every trip to the plate an adventure. Cramped conditions on the dilapidated team bus, with open windows serving as the air-conditioning and the smell of exhaust fumes ever present, make every road trip sickening.

The living style is reflective of the low salaries—players double up in rooms and some sleep four to an apartment to make ends meet. On the road, the team stays in clean, but unluxurious motels, paid for by the Seattle club.

"We eat a lot of hamburgers and pizzas," says one player about his daily nourishment. "What else can you do with $6.50 a day meal money?"

There are other costs involved with minor league life, of course. Each player is assessed clubhouse dues of $7 every two weeks, which covers the cleaning of his uniform. There is also the investment of a glove and spikes. A good infielder's glove will cost about $65, a top-line catcher's mitt $85. The average player wears out one glove and three pairs of shoes in a season.

Didier understands all of the agony of life in the minor leagues. He has been there himself, before hanging on as a backup catcher in the majors for parts or all of six seasons. He is, therefore, tolerant with his players. The twenty-nine-year-old manager seldom raises his voice while lecturing, and doesn't begrudge his players a good time. However, he comes down hard when a player's game suffers because of his off-the-field activities.

After another game with Salem, Didier and Pryor step out for a late-night drink and find two of the Bellingham players at the night spot, seated at a table next to the dance floor.

"Have a good time and enjoy yourself," Didier says to one of the players, outfielder Mike White. "But you better play hard tomorrow."

"I'm gonna play like an s. o. b.," promises White.

Didier knew he would.

6

A Clean, Well-Lighted Field

It is two hours before game time at sturdy Muzzy Field in Bristol, Conn., and already the hard-core fans have staked out their familiar places. Glazed by summer heat, they sprawl lazily in the stands and watch the leonine youths in knits crisply hit baseballs into the heavens and earth.

"Batting practice," says superfan Frank Lamb, "it's one of the best parts of the game."

If ever there is an all-star team for fans, Lamb might very well be the captain, for it was he who accounted for one of the most outrageous stories of fanaticism in Bristol baseball history. During one game, Lamb suffered a heart attack. "I didn't want to leave. I told them they would have to carry me out." Lamb lasted until the seventh inning—when, in fact, he was carried out and taken to a hospital.

Such, it would seem, is the essence of the minor

league baseball fan, whose attachments are nothing short of ferocious because of the intimacy of the game. Many are not only fans—but friends—of the players.

It is just this family feeling that has brought a gaggle of people from West Haven to watch their beloved Yankees play the hated Red Sox in an important series near the end of the 1978 Eastern League season. Among them is a group of girls, close friends of the West Haven players, and Mrs. Jean Kaas, widely acknowledged number one fan of the Yankee team. As if to certify her lofty position as Queen Mother of West Haven Yankee fans, the license plate on her car reads "Fan 1." "I must admit," says Mrs. Kaas, "that originally came from the West Haven high school hockey team. But now it holds true for the New Haven Yankees."

Mrs. Kaas had built part of her social world around the West Haven players—making an annual pilgrimage to Florida to watch them in spring training ("They always know I'm coming and save the same room for me") and rarely missing games during the season. She usually sees all the home games and travels to nearby places like Bristol and Waterbury, Conn., and Holyoke, Mass., whenever possible. She has even followed the team to Jersey City, N. J., and Reading, Pa., for an occasional game.

"I just love the kids," says Mrs. Kaas, a moon-faced matron with an easy smile. "Each year, I die of a broken heart when they leave, and you say the next group could never be the same. But it is—and you find yourself falling in love all over again with them."

Mrs. Kaas serves as the unofficial den mother for the Yankees and her house is a kind of West Haven Welcome Wagon at the start of each season. She invites new players over for Sunday dinners, featuring banquets of Swedish meatballs, turkey, or pork. ("I feel they're just young kids away from home and they don't eat well.") Mrs. Kaas's mothering instinct also extends to rooms for the players until they can get settled, as well as a loaning service which deals in heating pads, blankets, and hot water bottles. ("Rick Stenholm has been having trouble with his legs this season, and he still has my heating pad.") She also plays fisherman with the players, sinking lobster pots in front of her waterside home in league with Ron Davis and Mark Softy during the 1978 season. ("In six weeks, we caught thirty-five lobsters. We had a great time. It was something for them to do.")

"It's so important for them to have this type of relationship at the start of the season," Mrs. Kaas says. "When they first come into town, they're all lost, and they need friends and confidence-building. All their lives they've been treated as something special. But in professional ball, they're thrown into a situation where they're just another number. It has to be crushing to their egos."

Such relationships born in the fatiguing conditions of minor league life often blossom into lifelong friendships. Mrs. Kaas keeps up with many of the players after they leave West Haven, especially if they make the majors. Such as Ron Guidry, Larry Murray, Jim Beattie, Dell Alston, Terry Whitfield, and Scott MacGregor have made imprints on Mrs. Kaas's life. "I've visited them in Yankee Stadium," she says. "It was really a thrill for me to see them in that setting." She has gone to great lengths to visit her "boys"—once telling a guard at Yankee Stadium that she was the mother of one of them so she could get into a special visitors' area at the park. Murray was one of Mrs. Kaas's favorites.

"He taught me a good lesson about life," she says. "He had a marvelous attitude when he was struggling in the minors. He often used the word, 'whatever'—meaning whatever happens, happens. You can't worry about things. But he also said, 'I'll make it—don't worry.' Whatever—what a wonderful word. I've never forgotten that."

But the lesson is not always that easy for Mrs. Kaas to follow, especially in the stomach-churning days of a late-season pennant race. Passionately caught up in the Yankees' fight for the Eastern League pennant now, she confesses to an overkill of Rolaids for her nervous stomach. Things have not been going well for the West Haven Yankees of late, although they possess some of the best talent in the league, and a sweep of the two-game series in Bristol is imperative at this juncture of the season. "You're going to see a hungry ballclub in there tonight," Bristol Manager Tony Torchia had warned before the series started. It seemed he was right three hours later after the Yankees had belted the "Brisox" 9–4 behind the hitting of veteran Don Castle and the pitching of Chris Welch, a left-hander with a smooth motion that reminded observers of Don Gullett.

Like their counterparts in the big leagues, the Red Sox and Yankees draw well in the minors, too. For this game, 4,484 patrons attend on a promotional night, swelling the year's attendance over 52,000. The ring of the cash register on this August night is music to the ears of Bristol General Manager Charles Eshbach, whose hard work has given the Brisox credibility and some solid footing in town. In a couple of years in Bristol, he has overcome some tough problems—a stadium of low visibility in a setting away from the population center, miniscule parking facilities, and, perhaps most important of all, a divided city. "This town is very heavy into American Legion ball," explains Jack Lautier, a sportswriter for the *Bristol Press,* "and there's some small-minded jealousy among the Legion fans. Some think that the professional team has taken away the play from Legion ball, and the parents of the Legion players won't come to watch the Red Sox play."

However, there is a healthy group on hand for the second game of the West Haven series—among them, Mrs. Kaas and her husband, and the same group of West Haven girls who had been there the night before. "The thing that hurts these kids a lot of times," Mrs. Kaas is saying, "is their lack of confidence. They wouldn't be here without tools. They all have talent. But their mind destroys them very often. Take Ron Davis, the West Haven relief pitcher. He's the stopper here; you can count on him so much. But once when he was called up to the majors earlier this year to pitch for the Yankees, he was so nervous he couldn't throw the ball over the plate. It happened to be Oldtimers Day and people like Mickey Mantle, Joe DiMaggio, and Roger Maris were in the stands. They had to take him out of the game." (It was Davis, by the way, who secured the previous night's victory against Bristol with an inning of tidy relief.)

Although it is nearing game time, the atmosphere of Muzzy Field still presents the informality of an amateur game. Behind the stands, West Haven players, some still in grey sweat shirts and swinging towels over their heads, lean against the green fence and talk to family and admirers. On the field, the Bristol players entertain youngsters and anyone else who wishes to talk to them. They repeatedly sign autographs, pose for photographs, and joke with the crowd. Embraced by gargantuan trees in the outfield, courtesy of a picturesque city park, and high walls, Muzzy Field has been an appropriate place to watch professional baseball for some time. As they say, every seat in the house is a good one. ("The Bristol Owls used to play here in the old Colonial League," explains Eshbach, "but since then a number of changes have been made to this park. The grandstands used to be completely covered by wire —it looked like a chicken coop. They tore that down and put in bleachers. Now, we can squeeze in 4,500 sitting. We've had as much as 6,000 in here, though. They were lined three and four deep straight up the foul lines for one game last year.")

It is an ideal park for left-handed hitters, with the power alley in right-center (marked by a skinny light pole) beckoning only 330 feet away. Babe Ruth hit some prodigious home runs here, they say. Notes superfan Frank Lamb: "Ruth put a ball over the trees and into the swimming pool in the park. An old fellow claimed he found the ball floating in the water. That would make it about 700 feet!" (Ironically, though the park favors left-handers, the two best home run hitters seen at Bristol since the Red Sox put the franchise there six years ago were right-handers, Jim Rice and Jack Baker.)

"This is the best stadium in the league," says Lamb. "For one thing, there's a roof over many of the seats. It's clean, well-lighted, and one of the mildest places around to see a game. One time, they threw a drunk out. That was the most excitement I can remember happening in the stands."

The French National Anthem is played before the game, honoring a foreign visitor. But the record is cracked and goes on too long. The crowd fidgets, and the players in the Yankee dugout are laughing. Danny Parks, a short right-hander with flowing blond hair, takes the mound for Bristol, but obviously is not at his best. Jim McDonald, the burly West Haven first baseman, smashes a home run to friendly right-center field.

"Goodbye! Goodbye!" screams a joyful Mrs. Kaas, on her feet with her arms extended.

Later, she confides: "McDonald's got great tools, but he's a little bit of a showboat. That could hurt him."

Joe Lefebvre later also parks one. "He's my fa-vorite," Mrs. Kaas says as she watches the outfielder complete his trot back to the dugout for a drink of water. Close enough to converse freely with the players, Mrs. Kaas looks over to Lefebvre from her seat behind home plate and kids him. "Joe, that was, uh, so-so," she says, using her hands to indicate a blasé manner.

Mrs. Kaas also is a tough critic as well as a fan. When Yankee shortstop Domingo Ramos throws his helmet out of the dugout after being called out on a close play at first, the elder statesman of West Haven fans calls over harshly: "Grow up—you tur-key!"

The words seem incongruous with the lady's ap-pearance—she could be anybody's saintly mother or aunt—but they come tumbling out, nevertheless. Mrs. Kaas knows her baseball, all right, as well as her baseball players.

"Many of the Yankee kids pray to be traded," she offers. "They know they're stymied in the Yankee system what with all the talent up ahead of them. Dell Alston and Terry Whitfield were two of the best outfielders you could find in the minor leagues. They finally broke out of the system. But Alston was so depressed two years ago when he found out he had to go back to Syracuse for another year, he almost quit."

Mrs. Kaas's attachment to the players is no more fervent than the West Haven girls, seated nearby. They express the many faces of love. More than camp followers, they are friends and virtual sisters to the West Haven Yankees.

"We try to be their friends," notes Joanne Bruno, "because we know they need them." On this night, Miss Bruno is accompanied by Millie and Cathy Grollinger, Lois Siraco, and Linda McCarty. "I've sewn their uniforms," adds Joanne. "Once, I had to do a job for Jim McDonald when he ripped his pants stretching for a throw at first. He's a big fellow, you know." Millie Grollinger is the hairdresser in the group, and has styled many of the Yankee heads.

"Most of these guys just live for baseball," Miss Bruno says. "Paul Semall, for instance, is so dedicated that he goes to sleep early every night, eats steaks, and won't talk on the phone the day he's going to pitch. He doesn't even want to know when you're going to be at a game. He doesn't want to be distracted. It's everything to him. He wants to win so badly—it's his life."

The girls have befriended the umpires as well and find their dedication doubly passionate.

"The umpires hustle the same way the players do," notes Millie Grollinger. "They want to make it to the big leagues as much as the players do. They talk about it more."

The girls have found the umpiring breed to be different than the players, though. "The umpires are far more 'straighter' than the players," says one girl. "They don't drink or smoke pot. They're 'safer,' more fatherly, and treat me like a sister. You wouldn't believe how good the umpires are! And they really think the players are scum—womanizers, playboys. They hate the ballplayers."

The girls feel the umpires are wrong about this, of course. They attribute more noble characteristics to their young heroes, one pointing out: "Why, the team pitched in $5 each to allow the bat boy, Derrick Rogers, to go on this current road trip. They're really great people."

The late innings feature some thunder from Bristol bats. It is Rolaids time now for Mrs. Kaas. "Oh, dear," she says, watching the usually peerless Ron Davis fail to hold a West Haven lead in the ninth. The Red Sox eventually go on to win and split the two-game series, hurting the Yankee pennant chances. (As it turns out, Bristol—the winner of the first-half pennant race—becomes the eventual Eastern League champion by beating Reading in the playoffs.)

But there will always be a next year for people like Mrs. Kaas and the other members of the West Haven Yankee sorority. "I'm already preparing myself to fall in love with a new group," Mrs. Kaas says, waving on her way out of the stadium.

7

Return of "Supernuck"

"I flipped on the radio and instead of that Top 40 stuff I found an all-night, oldies but goodies station. I sang to those good old songs all the way from Savannah to Atlanta. Five and a half hours! It was like I was driving to Emerald City."—Jim Bouton after his recall to the major leagues in the late summer of 1978.

Yes, it was just like driving to see the Wizard of Oz in the Emerald City, Jim Bouton thought as he took the trip from Savannah to Atlanta that fine summer night. Only in this case, the "Wizard" was Ted Turner, owner of the Atlanta Braves and one of the prize eccentrics in baseball. And Bouton was anything but the Cowardly Lion. Actually, he had proved himself to be somewhat of a hero in his latest role—the champion of baseball's senior citizen set and a shining image for anyone who ever dreamed impossible dreams.

Bouton's Yellow Brick Road to Atlanta was paved by the annual September swell of big league rosters—the quaint custom by which major league teams enlarge their companies from twenty-five to forty men in the season's last month. Most of these callow September people are promoted from the minors as a token gesture, allowed to swagger on big league ballfields in innocuous roles. Few make the kind of noises Bouton made upon his return to the big time in September of 1978.

The first time Bouton stepped on a major league diamond after eight years' absence, they asked him to try to stop the Los Angeles Dodgers, one of baseball's premier teams. Bouton was juggling magic numbers in his glove—the Dodgers were going hard for the National League West pennant.

"It might as well be the Dodgers," he said rather boldly. "When you're rolling the dice you might as well go for the big numbers."

Other men had returned to the majors at Bouton's age, which was thirty-nine, but none had been out of the game for so many years, entered other careers, or had exchanged old bodies for new. Bouton was 20 pounds lighter than when he had pitched for the Houston Astros in 1970, a desultory effort. He was aware that this major league reincarnation was not a total salute to his pitching prowess. He was brought in to stir up flagging interest.

"As far as hyping the gate," he said, "a lot of people will come to see me because of what I've accomplished, and I think it's justified."

Just what had Bouton accomplished? Just about everything, that's all.

At one time he had been king of the hill with the New York Yankees—a hard-throwing right-hander who could throw a ball through the proverbial brick wall. That irresistible fastball helped him forge a 21–7 record for the American League champion Yankees in 1963 and an 18–13 mark and two World Series victories in 1964. Then, just like that, the arm went and so did Bouton's baseball career for the moment.

As subsequent events would show, each time Bouton is knocked down by one of life's inside hard ones, he only bounces back higher the next time. In this case, it was a best-selling book called *Ball Four* that got him up off the floor and put him in major league literary circles. With that powerful book, he traded simple baseball fame for notoriety. He became a television sportscaster in New York and proved so naturally glib that he was asked to appear on TV shows such as "What's My Line" alongside such personalities as Arlene Francis and Bill Cullen. Then he did some acting in a situation comedy based on his best-seller.

But all the while he was on television, Bouton ached to be on another stage, the baseball diamond. It was not just a quixotic daydream. His fastball was gone, true. But he was developing a formidable knuckleball and luxuriated in his whimsical nickname, "Supernuck." Flirting with the notion of escaping back to the diamond almost every day since he left the sport in 1970, Bouton began his comeback try in modest surroundings at first. He kept pitching semipro baseball, and dragged his family off to pitching vacations in Oregon and Canada. Once, Bouton and some friends even considered buying their own minor league team so he could be assured of a pitching job.

"I remember when I first quit TV to go back to baseball, everybody said I was crazy," Bouton remembers.

It seemed crazy, of course, to everyone but Jim Bouton. He was risking embarrassment and the financial well-being of his family. But to Bouton's wife, Bobby, her husband's mental well-being was more important than anything. He was obviously going through some kind of middle-age life crisis, and she wanted to help him with that. "I'd feel terrible if we held him back," she explained. "Of course it's been tough on me. I miss him very much. It's hard. But whether or not what Jim is doing is fair to me or the children doesn't matter, because for now he's doing what I want him to do."

Bouton's full-time comeback began in 1977 in Bill Veeck's Chicago White Sox farm system. Even though Bouton had agreed to pay all of his expenses, only two major league teams would grant him any audience. The comeback trail was strewn with thorns: an 0–6 record at the Double-A level in Knoxville and 1–4 at Triple-A in Durango, Mexico. Finally he had some success at the Single-A level, a 5–1 record in Portland, and that gave him some inspiration. He cashed in his children's college savings, sold an expensive home and bought a more modest one, and worked out all winter at a college gym. Then he found an angel in Ted Turner in the summer of 1978 and Bouton, as towheaded and shiny-faced as any rookie, showed up to pitch batting practice for meal money at Atlanta's Triple-A farm team in Richmond.

The ever-inventive Turner, a throwback to Bill Veeck, baseball's past-master of entertainment, saw a splendid opportunity to make hay when the Atlanta Braves visited Richmond for an exhibition game. Turner had two ideas: he would umpire third and Bouton would pitch. Coincidentally, Turner, too, was thirty-nine years old.

"It was my greatest day in a baseball uniform," Bouton says. "I never had more pressure, because if I didn't come through, I was gone. You lose in a World Series, you'll still be a starter next spring. I hadn't pitched in competition for a month and nobody would let me throw my knuckler in batting practice. And I walked out on that mound cold, and I stuck it to the Atlanta Braves before 13,000 people. They got one run off me in six innings, and I struck out seven of them."

Bouton sighs.

"That night was magic. I've had other great moments, but that night I felt I was omnipotent, and once you've done that you've got to think that you can be magic again."

Turner obviously thought so, because he hired him to pitch in earnest for his Savannah farm team in the Class AA Southern League. Bouton worked harder than any rookie half his age. The passion was there, if sometimes the pitching wasn't. Bouton was successful in his first start, but his second was a disaster. After giving up six runs in 5⅓ innings in a 6-5 loss to Orlando on May 24, Bouton had nothing left but his humor to fall back on: "I wasn't quite with it. If I had been doing the cha-cha, I would have been stepping on my partner's toes."

He also had his philosophy.

"People have got to understand—I want to get to the highest level of competition I possibly can, but I swear I am not trying to get to the majors. It's sort of like Zen. I don't want to aim for the target. The way to hit it is not to aim for it. All I know is that this experience has been satisfying in every respect. It is even satisfying when I don't win. So I know I've made the right decision whether or not I ever get any higher. I've been happy most of my life, but never more than now. Of course, the minors are not as good as the majors, but the question to me is whether the minors are better than much of the rest of life. And to me, they are."

Bouton's Impossible Dream had been so painfully intense at this point that no one could have suggested that he was just researching another book. "Someday I may want to do a book," he said. "But I have absolutely no intention of doing so now. I wouldn't want a book as a saving thing. I'd lose the fun of the experience if I had that to fall back on. If with each setback, I could say, 'Well, it really doesn't matter because it's another good chapter,' then the experience itself would be devalued."

But if Bouton was something of an idealist, he also began to look something like a pitcher in subsequent appearances. Using only a knuckleball, mixed in with an occasional palm ball and slowed-down fastball, Bouton began pitching with consistency. By mid-August, he owned a 6–5 record with a 3.58 earned-run average and had hurled three shutouts, including a one-hit beauty. Probably just as important to Bouton himself was the fact that he had finished seven games in eleven starts. Bouton likes finishing things he starts.

At this point, Bouton had a lot of rooters behind him, and not only those that sat in the stands. "There wasn't a player on the team that didn't talk up for Jim, who didn't want him to show all the doubters what he can do," said Stu Livingstone, a Savannah relief pitcher. Bill Lucas, director of player personnel for the Atlanta Braves, was also a big fan of Bouton's. As was Savannah Manager Bobby Dews after he witnessed his fine human drama. Said Lucas: "He's trying to perfect a new pitch, and he will have his moments. He hasn't got it down to perfection yet. But he's done all we could ask of a Class AA pitcher. And he's working his butt off to make it." Dews believed Bouton could jump all the way back to the top. "Most knuckleball pitchers have more movement on the ball than Jim does," he said. "But when Jim's is working, it's really good—good enough to get him back into the majors."

Although no other player on the roster of the Savannah Braves had yet reached the age of twenty-five, Bouton fit in better with this crew than he did in his glory days with the Yankees. Then he was viewed as something of an odd duck, a peculiar fellow because he read books, made jewelry, and roomed with Latin players so he could help them and improve his Spanish. Today's players, who read his antiestablishment *Ball Four* in their growing-up years, would probably tend to accept and identify with his vibrant individuality, in this the Age of Aquarius.

While Bouton was having a grand old time of it, though, his wife had to shoulder the heavier responsibilities of home.

"I will admit the person who suffers in all of this is Bobby," said Bouton at the time. "For whatever benefit this may be for the kids, she's the one left alone to take care of them. But I feel a need to be away from my family for awhile right now. I need to be by myself at this point in my life. Look, I'm in my mid-life crisis. This is all part of that. It's more than just wanting to pitch. It's wanting to prepare myself for the rest of my life. When [the show] "Ball Four" was canceled, I had a lot of good options, but my body told me to play ball again. My body knows more about me than my conscious mind. On the mound, my instincts have often determined for me what pitch I should throw. It was those feelings that told me to pitch again."

The Savannah Braves not only took advantage of Bouton's pitching abilities, but also his box-office potential. He had opened in Savannah in a blaze of national attention before an unusually large crowd —an inventive management let a fan in free if he brought a copy of *Ball Four* with him. Whenever and wherever Bouton pitched, crowds swelled past the usual size, and the senior citizen of the Savannah Braves heard warm and telling applause, win or lose. But he did win more than he lost, posting a 12–9 record and a 2.77 earned-run average for the season.

Effective on the mound and at the gate, Bouton was a September natural for the Atlanta Braves, who sorely needed help in both departments. "Bill [Lucas] called me and said I was pitching Sunday against the Los Angeles Dodgers," Bouton said, recalling the magic moment of his promotion to the major leagues. "It seemed a little ridiculous to me . . ." The call came on a Thursday, so Bouton had some time to meditate on this incredible stroke of luck. "Who'd have thought I'd get this far?" he said. His modesty, however, was soon overshadowed by a steel-like self-belief—a trait that had carried him through hard times before. "Maybe I could end up winning fifteen to twenty games—who knows?" he said. "No one has ever tested the limits to see how long a knuckleball pitcher can go. I just know that only Ted Turner and maybe Charlie Finley or Bill Veeck would have enough imagination to give a thirty-nine-year-old pitcher a chance."

As Bouton prepared to join a team of big-league strangers, he added this postscript.

"Whatever happens, this has been the most satisfying summer of my life. Two years ago I would dream of this moment, putting on a major league uniform again, and in my daydreams I would always see myself crying. But when the moment came, it

116

was different. I can't explain my emotions, because they're different from what anyone has ever had. But my perceptions have changed. Two years ago it was a dream. But I have earned this uniform. What I accomplished this summer was a reality. I belong here. I'm a bona fide major leaguer. I didn't have to cry."

There were some who disagreed with Bouton's assessment of himself. Some cheerless critics from the Dodgers and Cincinnati Reds, for instance, were not as receptive to the romance of the moment as was the crowd of 11,162 which stood and applauded the man as he stepped to the mound at Atlanta Stadium. "It's a joke," Dodger outfielder Reggie Smith said. "At some point Ted Turner is going to have to stop making fun of this game." Davey Lopes, the Los Angeles second baseman, was disturbed by the "circuslike atmosphere." Cincinnati Manager Sparky Anderson filed a protest with Baseball Commissioner Bowie Kuhn and in so many words called Bouton's appearance a disgrace to baseball.

Bouton certainly did nothing to be ashamed of in the early going. He got the side out in order in the first, and through three innings gave up only one walk. But the dream ended in the fourth, when he lost some of his rhythm and got a little wild. Warming up before the game, Bouton was aware he had only a pedestrian knuckler that day. In his last start in the Southern League, he had pitched a two-hitter against Orlando with a gorgeous knuckleball—"supernuck," Bouton had said. Then he threw the pitch 95 percent of the time. But it didn't behave as well against the Dodgers and he had to mix in his palm ball and a "cut" fastball (timed at a hardly formidable 70 miles per hour) and an occasional changeup. After a walk to Bill North, Steve Garvey got the Dodgers' first hit. Two more singles followed and then Rick Monday hit a three-run homer for a 5-1 Dodger lead. Trailing 6-1, Bouton went out for a pinch-hitter after five innings, but wasn't discouraged. He was, in fact, elated.

"I think I proved my stuff is good enough," he said. "It's only a matter of being consistent. I did it. I came all the way back, and I got out big league hitters."

"Butterflies" fluttered like the knuckler inside Bouton from the start, but the moment was more critically attuned to the heart than the stomach. "I'm in a territory nobody's ever been to before," he said. "There are so many shouldn'ts and can'ts in the world that when someone challenges them, as I have, and beats them, as I have, then it has to inspire people."

Bouton considered the day a victory, even though it was a defeat in baseball terms that left his major league lifetime record at 61-61. He would improve that later in September with a victory over the San Francisco Giants, but that wasn't the important thing. What the heck—he had already been to the Emerald City; he had already made the trip all the way back.

The pride of the Yankees, minor-league version, is evident in the banner over Main Street in Oneonta, N.Y.

ABOVE: Oneonta's quaint Damaschke Field, a classic setting for a minor league baseball game.
BELOW: The game has everyone's rapt attention at Damaschke—fans and players alike.

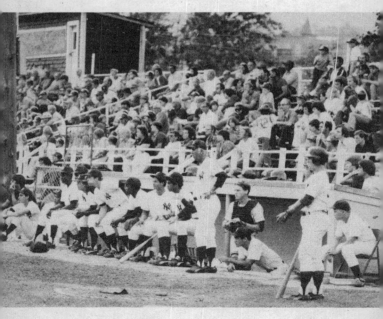

The mountains loom in left field, a wondrous
backdrop for baseball at Damaschke Field.

ABOVE: Brian Ryder delivers one of his high, hard ones for the Oneonta Yankees. *BELOW:* A winning team in Oneonta—owner Sam Nader (left) and manager Art Mazmanian. *Oneonta Yankees photo.*

The pregame scene at Muzzy Field in Bristol,
Connecticut—boys and girls together.

Bristol's boy of summer, Tony Torchia, stands a lonely vigil in the third-base coaching box.

ABOVE: The line forms for a big game at Muzzy Field between the Bristol Red Sox and West Haven Yankees, two of the Eastern League's hottest rivals.
BELOW: The game is played in the dugout, too—in this case, the West Haven Yankees.

Game action between West Haven and Bristol at tree-lined Muzzy Field.

Mike O'Berry (left) and Tom Farrias, two of the many minor leaguers who dream of glory.

Roosevelt Stadium in Jersey City—more people on the field than in the stands.

Two of McKoy Stadium's biggest features—Ben Mondor and the murals. *Henry F. Mathews photo.*

ABOVE: Pawtucket's proud showplace for baseball, McKoy Stadium, lights up on a late summer night.
BELOW: A Rochester Red Wing slides home safely in an International League game at Pawtucket.
Henry F. Mathews photo.

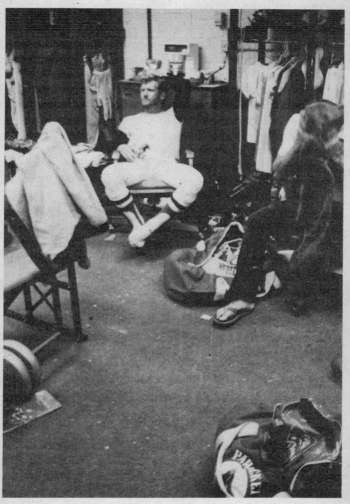
Locker room contemplation at McKoy Stadium.
Henry F. Mathews photo.

Creative Pat McKernan, a first-class minor league showman.

A man for all seasons and reasons—Jim Bouton.
Bob Morris, SAVANNAH NEWS.

True grit, minor-league style in El Paso, Texas.
El Paso Diablos photo.

8

A Tale of Three Managers

Joe Morgan's legends precede him.

"Are they all true?" a visitor asks the manager of the Pawtucket Red Sox.

"Name some, and I'll tell you."

"The one with you standing face-to-face with the umpire and not saying a word for twenty minutes while 16,000 fans in Columbus went bananas?"

"Yes, but I might say it was more like thirty seconds."

"You were arrested for that, right?"

"*Arrested!* I've never been arrested in my life! I was, uh, ushered off the field by some policemen. My case was arrested to the clubhouse."

"What about the Dick Sharon thing, where you went out to center field to shake his hand in the middle of a game after he made three great catches in a space of four outs?"

"Yeah, that happened. It was here, at Pawtucket. The guy made three fabulous diving catches out of four outs, and I just had to go out and shake his hand. You'll never see it again. The point is, how many times are you going to get three diving catches like that in that space of time by the same man? They've got to hit you three of the same type balls in the same place out of four outs. It's unbelievable!"

There are other bizarre Joe Morgan stories to fill the ears, most of them emanating from his theatrical flair in dealing with umpires.

"What is your modus operandi for umpires? Do you try to antagonize them?"

Morgan wrinkles his hawkish nose as if to say, "What kind of a question is that?" Then he says it all.

"No, my modus operandi is you're trying to win and if they make a bad call, you let them know about it. Case closed! Next day it's another start."

In the ultraconservative society of baseball, Joe Morgan is surely a refreshing breeze—adding a dash of color to a sport often burdened by gray matter. His eccentric, appealing behavior, however, is not the reason that he's currently managing the Boston Red Sox' top farm team in the Triple-A International League. Morgan happens to be one of the most astute baseball minds in the business, as well as one of the best leaders of men.

"If you can't play for Joe Morgan," says veteran Pawtucket second baseman Buddy Hunter, "you can't play for anybody. He goes out and fights for you. He thinks about his players. I've been playing for Joe for four years now and I haven't heard a bad thing said about him."

Other player testimonials abound and Morgan also has the acknowledgment of greatness from baseball society itself. He has twice won manager of the year awards in the minors, once in the Pittsburgh Pirate chain and in 1977 when he led Pawtucket to the International League pennant. Morgan is modest about his achievements, though. "You try to win and get the guys ready for the majors at the same time. You don't have to pick out the prospects. By the time they get here, they can either do it or they can't. Jim Rice and Fred Lynn, I didn't have to do anything for them—just let them play."

But make no mistake about it—there are tricks to managing, and Morgan knows them all. While all that golden Red Sox talent is flowing through his hands at Pawtucket, he still has to polish it. Motivation, he finds, is his toughest job.

"The hardest thing," he says, "is trying to beat it into these guys what this game is all about. You have to stay on them over and over, telling them the same things and try to get them to work on their weaknesses, which they don't particularly like to do. If a guy's a good hitter, he's up there swinging the bat all day long. Some of them can't catch a cold, and they should be trying to better themselves defensively. One way or other, you have to motivate them. You have to kid around with them sometimes and other times you have to lay it on the line to them. You have to keep them thinking. They fall asleep a lot. When you play every day, it's tough to stay alive. You go out there ten days in a row, you probably only really feel like playing five or six. But what happens to the other four? That's where the manager comes in. He's got to notice these things and wake these guys up."

If anyone can do it, Morgan can. His dialogue is always straight and lucid. Ask him who has a chance to make it and who hasn't, and he'll tell you. Ask him why others keep trying, and he'll tell you that, too. "Hell, if we told everyone who couldn't make it to go home, we'd have no players at all," he says.

To "make it," of course, means the big leagues. Morgan is trying like everyone else.

"We're all in the same boat," he says. "We're all looking to move up. I look at it that sometime I'll get a chance, whether it's a coach or a manager. Naturally, I'd rather be the manager. But there is no place like the big leagues, when you get right down to it ... especially when you're getting along in years and you'd like to build up some pension. I'm forty-eight now."

Whenever the Boston Red Sox falter and Manager Don Zimmer becomes unpopular, Morgan's name usually comes up as a replacement.

"I knew Zimmer would be the next manager the day they hired him as a third base coach," says Morgan. "We both applied for that job. He got it. I came here ... that's the way it goes."

Morgan is not out to bump Zimmer, however. Morgan is a loyalist, professing to bleed Red Sox Red.

"I hope Zimmer wins every game," says the Pawtucket manager. "I'm a Soxer all the way."

That fierce loyalty, by the way, seems to be indigenous to the entire Red Sox farm system—one of the reasons that it is one of the finest around.

"We're proud of our guys," says Morgan, flexing his Boston Red Sox look-alike cap with a "P" in front. "Almost everyone on the field up there in the majors as a regular was a member of our farm system. You've got to give the people along the way credit. We've got some good minor league managers in this system . . . guys who work hard. The guys are interested in baseball, number one, and put a lot into it. I've been impressed by some of our lower-level guys . . . the amount of time they put into their work."

While serving as Zimmer's alter ego in 1978, Morgan was in some pretty good company in the International League. Ken Boyer managed Rochester before he moved up to the majors and was replaced by Frank Robinson, once an irresistible major leaguer. Cal Ermer, who had a stint as manager of the Minnesota Twins, handled Toledo. And former big leaguer Johnny Lipon managed Columbus. On almost every roster, as well, was a name that registered in a baseball fan's memory. At Richmond, it was the name of pitching coach Johnny Sain, subject of the old Boston Braves' refrain, "Spahn and Sain and a day of rain."

"I suppose I have all my life to wait for my chance," Morgan reflects philosophically. "Most of these kids will quit if they don't get to the majors in a few years."

Actually, Morgan has been in a minor league holding pattern for an impressive amount of time already. He started managing in the Pittsburgh Pirate chain in 1966 before joining the Red Sox organization in the 1970s. Before that, he played in the system of the old Boston Braves, signing in 1952 out of Boston College, and except for a few years as a fill-in player in the big leagues, spent most of his time at the Triple-A level.

"Back then," says Morgan, "a guy had been playing six to seven years when he got to Triple-A (from rookie leagues through Classes D, C, A, and AA). Now they get here after only playing two, three years, and they are far from polished."

Morgan espouses the theory that the old days were better in terms of quantity of better players.

"The good players today are as good as the good ones then—there just aren't as many. Just think how many didn't make it when there were sixteen major league franchises and fifty-six different minor leagues. [Now there are twenty-six major league teams and less than twenty leagues in the minors.] There are 2,000 fewer kids playing in the minors now. To me, there doesn't seem to be that many good players coming out of Double-A anymore."

Morgan adds whimsically: "Anyone who made it then could stay around now forever."

It is the popular theory that the modern major leagues have been "watered down" by expansion and that overall quality is not up to the standards of earlier times. Morgan is passionately supportive of this notion.

"I could name a lot of guys in the big leagues today that I thought would never get there," he says. "But with expansion, they eventually made it. I think you have to lower your standards quite a bit today. Everyone in Triple-A still has an outside chance of getting there. There's been a lot of injuries lately, too, it seems. There's a guy in Atlanta, Chico Ruiz, who has been in this league for a long time and last year didn't even have a regular job at Richmond. But now he's in the big leagues, because they had injuries. Chico probably never thought he'd see the majors again."

The interview with Morgan takes place in his cramped office, not much larger than a walk-in closet, in the bowels of concrete McCoy Stadium. The manager speaks softly, hunched forward with his hands clasped, and unruffled by obscenities bellowed by Pawtucket players through paper-thin walls. Morgan is a likeable man with sandy-colored hair and sharp features and possibly could pass for a policeman on the beat. A barely discernible New England accent flavors his speech, and he is consistently firm in his judgments—the mark of a good leader. Now he is talking about some of his favorite players, singling one out especially as a surefire major leaguer. You listen with respect to a man who has boosted the stars of such as Jim Rice, Fred Lynn, Rick Burleson, and Butch Hobson.

"Gary Allenson, the catcher, has been a shining star for us this year," Morgan says. "He hit better than I thought he'd hit; his catching and throwing have improved since opening day. He's going to be ready for the big leagues next year. Of course, he'll be a backup to Carlton Fisk. I think this guy can do it."

It is with special pride that Morgan underscores Allenson, a muscular youngster with a marvelous arm who was able to pick more than twenty runners off first base during the 1978 season. Allenson was regarded as a second choice by most of the Red Sox minor league officials, who preferred to promote Bristol's Mike O'Berry to Pawtucket for the 1978 season. But Morgan opted for Allenson, even though he was with a lower minor league affiliate, at Winter Haven of the Class A Florida State League.

"I liked his bat, his bat speed, and I figured he would come around as a catcher," Morgan explains. "So I took him, and it's worked out great." (Allenson wound up hitting in the vicinity of .300 for the season and excelled defensively, while O'Berry had a comparatively desultory season at Bristol, Boston's Double-A affiliate.)

Such personal triumphs are the lifeblood of managing at the minor league level, where there are always more hardships than hurrahs. Even in the Triple-A International League—the jet-set level of the minors—life can be a bit strained.

"There aren't enough off-days in the minors," notes Morgan, "and it really keeps you hopping. We only have about three or four days off from the opening gun to the end, and that's not really enough. In the big leagues, they're off at least one day a week—and sometimes more than that. Also, the travel is a bit tough when you have to make plane connections. Everytime we go on a road trip from here, we get up about five o'clock in the morning because you have to be in New York or some other big city at seven to catch the better flight. You go up and down a lot."

Morgan copes, better than most, and contributes an individual flair to his art.

"Morgan is a legendary manager," emphasizes Ben Mondor, the garrulous owner of the Pawtucket team. "After spring training, we have meetings with the umpires and league presidents to go over things such as rules, new adaptations. I was talking to one of the presidents of the leagues and he was telling me, 'You know, you fellows ruin these meetings— half the day is spent telling Joe Morgan stories by all the umpires!'"

Ah, yes, the stories.

"Morgan will liven up a game for you," Mondor says. "He's been known to give the fans a little show. You will see a play happen and Joe Morgan rush right out, come charging across the field like the world was coming to an end. He gets close to an umpire, throws his own cap off, and sticks a finger in the ump's face and looks like he's giving him hell. And the crowd roars and the fans say how come he never gets thrown out? He always does that on opposing fields. But do you know what he says when he gets out on the field? He puts out the finger and says, '*You're right*!' Now the crowd thinks he's telling the umpires something else entirely and wants him thrown out. But how can they throw him out for saying, 'You're right.' Of course, the people can't hear what he's saying. They see gestures and imagine all kinds of four-letter words."

Morgan stories spring eternally. Buddy Hunter, who has played for Morgan more seasons than anyone on the current Pawtucket roster, offers, "He's done some crazy things, all right. One time one of our players was called out on a slide into second base and Morgan went out to argue the call. They were all standing around first when all of a sudden, Morgan takes off running and makes a perfect hook slide into second base. He wanted to demonstrate his point . . . but the umpire didn't appreciate it and kicked him out.

"Another time, there was a man on first base for the other team and our pitcher threw over there about five times in a row. Each time he threw to first, it was very close and Joe thought he was out all five times. The sixth time he threw over there, Joe came running out of the dugout. Our first baseman gave the 'safe' sign to Joe, but that didn't stop him from coming out. He ran up to the umpire and said to his face, 'What was he?' The umpire said, 'Joe, he was safe.' Then Joe said, 'You're damn right he was!' and turned and went back to the dugout and just left the umpire hanging there. The umpire didn't know what to think."

The Dick Sharon story has been told and retold in a variety of minor league citadels, and is as characteristic as any of Morgan's legendary feats.

"I was playing second base at the time," Hunter remembers, "and Sharon was in center field for us. Sharon made three of the best catches you'll see within four outs and all of a sudden I see Joe Morgan running out of the dugout and heading toward center field. I turned around and thought, gee, maybe Dick was injured or something. But Sharon was standing up, and seemed to be okay. Joe Morgan went up to him and said, 'That was the three best catches I've ever seen. You're not that good.' Then he shook his hand and ran back to the dugout . . . right in the middle of a game."

Hunter shook his head.

"Joe Morgan," he said, "will keep you loose."

As is his custom, Tony Torchia is out at the park early this windless, sky-blue day. It is a fine moment for baseball and the manager of the Bristol Red Sox appears to be reliving some fantasies of youth. He is still a boy of summer. He stands on the mound, half-dressed in his uniform, and pitches batting practice for some youngsters. He winds up like Sandy Koufax and sends up soft pitches. The youngsters swing like Willie Mays and hit them to the outer reaches of the field. Do all old minor league first basemen end up this way? Only if you're lucky, says Torchia.

"When you've spent as much time as I have in the minor leagues," he says, "it's best to do it with an organization like the Boston Red Sox. The Red Sox treat players like human beings. They've always been good to me."

The Red Sox repay loyalty. In Torchia's case, they

gave him a manager's job after thirteen distinguished years of service as a player in their minor league system. Two years of good work at Winston-Salem, a Class A affiliate, demanded his promotion to the Double-A Eastern League team at Bristol in 1978. There he won the pennant and more applause from the Red Sox brass.

"Actually," Torchia says modestly, "it isn't very hard to manage. You could make it hard if you expect all your players to play like big leaguers, and get mad and fine them and chew them out. But I'm not like that. I try to put as little pressure on them as I can, so I can get the most out of them. The kids are a lot more sensitive these days than when I was playing. It seems they could take criticism a little better back then . . ."

So Torchia speaks softly and lets his players carry the big sticks.

"I try to treat them like men," says Torchia. "I want them to have as much control over their own destinies as they can. That is what is going to get them to the major leagues. I can't kick a guy in the butt for 140 games and then a Triple-A manager will kick him in the butt for 140 games and then somebody in the big leagues will kick him for ten years. It doesn't work that way; a guy has to have enough inner desire to do it himself. I just try to expose the game to him, teach him as much as I can, and help him develop the right attitude."

Torchia relaxes now in the dugout at Bristol's Muzzy Field, watching his young gladiators at serious pregame work. His conversation is interrupted by occasional business. ("Hey, Group C, hey, Julio, that's enough!" he shouts to his shortstop, Julio Valdez, indicating an end to infield practice. Or, to the manager of the West Haven Yankees: "Hey, Stump, we may be hitting earlier today, so you'll have more time for batting practice." Carl "Stump" Merrill spits out some tobacco juice and nods all in the same motion.)

The subject of managing gets more play from Torchia.

"The hardest thing," he says, "is getting my players to play as a team all the time, because they know that the whole team is not going to move up. They're in it for themselves a lot of the time because they're trying to get to the big leagues. Once you're in the big leagues, making the money, you can be a lot better team player. You're there, and you're trying to win. Here, guys worry about their own careers too much when they go bad. They feel they might not make it, and lose track of the team ... and it hurts the team and themselves. I try to get them to think about the team. I know if they do that, it will help them as individuals."

Torchia leans his head against the dugout's concrete wall, stretching his feet out so they rest on the steps. He watches his players as he talks.

"You know, a lot of baseball is in the head," he says. "The psychological aspects of this game are tremendous. There's been a lot of examples of guys who tore up the minor leagues and the first time they went to the majors, they couldn't do it and had to go back. Bill Robinson is one. So is Joe Rudi. And

Gene Tenace . . . John Mayberry. They didn't adjust. They were batting against guys they had read about all their lives and they lost faith in themselves."

Torchia smiles.

"Then there were others who had mediocre years in the minors and once they got to the big leagues, weren't going to let it pass. Carlton Fisk is one of those . . . and so is Freddy Lynn. They asked Lynn why he only hit .280 in Triple-A and why he was the Most Valuable Player in the American League the next year and he said, 'Well, I just saw 35,000 fans up there every day and it did something to me. At Pawtucket, we only had 350.' He had the ability, but the fans and the intensity of the big leagues brought more of it out of him."

Success in the Eastern League doesn't necessarily mean quick passage to the majors—as Torchia's ill-fated career proved—but it is a standard of excellence in the minors. Several players have gone straight to the big leagues from the classy Double-A league, or needed no more than a few finishing touches in Triple-A on the way up. The Eastern League has been one of the best proving grounds for major leaguers because of its unique demands on hitters.

"It's very cold the first month and the infields are real soft in the East," says Torchia. "Also, a lot of the lights aren't very good because a lot of the parks are old. So those are three big factors that really lower the batting averages." (Torchia led the league once with a .294 average.)

The playing conditions are better out West, of course.

"The Texas League, for instance, is real dry and the ball carries good. The infield is real hard and the ball shoots through there. It's warm from the opening day. You know that a hitter has to play every day, and the first month here you only play about four or five days a week and then you have a couple of days off because of the rain. You lose your timing. If you shifted every one from the Texas League and put them in the Eastern League and put all of us in the Texas League, the averages would be the same for the league. In other words, the .330 hitter there would hit .290 or .300 here. Same with the International League and the Pacific Coast League. Every year, I used to watch the batting averages and I would count down the first forty hitters . . . and the fortieth hitter in the Coast League would be hitting .290 and the fortieth hitter in the International League would be hitting .260. And I know the Coast League is no better. The pitching's no better, because the minor league teams are switching franchises constantly, moving in and out of leagues. Still, the averages stay the same. It's the same thing there—soft infields, bad lights, and a lot of rotten weather in the East. The Coast League has newer ballparks, faster infields . . . just better conditions."

Awareness of such subtleties adds a new dimension to the already-profound complexities of minor league managing.

"You have to know the parks," Torchia says. "West Haven has a fence in right field that's really short, about 295 feet. They're way ahead of everyone in home runs and forty points higher in batting average. If I'm the West Haven manager, and a guy hits a 300-foot homer, when I call in the game that night, I say he hit a home run, but it wasn't really a homer. At the end of the year, a guy might have thirty home runs, and people think he has a lot of power. But if I have to recommend him for Tacoma [the New York Yankees' Triple-A team], I would say, wait a minute, he only hit seven of them really good, so don't expect that much power from him at Tacoma. Now he might not even make the team."

Torchia excuses himself for a half-minute to talk to a player. Now he is back.

"The thing is, I never look at statistics when I size up a player. I might have a pitcher who is one-and-ten and I might still feel he's going to be in Boston in three years because he throws good, but they haven't made the plays behind him here. If he gets to the big leagues, there will be big leaguers making big league plays behind him. The regular statistics might mean a lot to a kid getting a raise, but a guy who hits .320 might not be any more of a prospect than a guy who hits .280. It's just how they hit the ball. Maybe a guy is hitting line drives that are being caught every night and the other guy is hitting bloopers and he ends up hitting thirty points higher . . . but he's not necessarily a better prospect."

Torchia's main job, of course, is developing players for the Boston Red Sox. Winning minor league pennants, as glamorous as it might seem, is a secondary consideration for the parent team. However, this does not stop Torchia from feeling pain in losses—or softly cursing the Red Sox for stealing key figures at crucial times of the season and filling Bristol's roster with too many "wrong-side" hitters. It is one of the most common problems, and one of the toughest to overcome, in minor league managing.

"Our ballpark is conducive to left-hand hitters," Torchia explains, "but of course we have nothing but right-handers here because Boston recruits that way for Fenway Park. Boston naturally signs four or five right-hand hitters for every left-hand hitter. We'd like to have a couple of good lefties in the line-up, but naturally they're looking for someone to hit it over their fence in left field. It doesn't hurt me as far as player development is concerned—if a guy can hit it over the fence here, he can hit it over the 'Green Monster' in Boston. But it does matter to me as far as our won-lost record is concerned."

Midway through the summer, after Bristol had won the first-half EL pennant, Torchia was stripped of three of his better players—pitcher Bob Sprowl, and outfielders Otis Foster and Ken Huizenga. Their promotion to Pawtucket in the International League did wonders for their careers, but not much for the second-half hopes of the Bristol team. However, after floundering in August, the Red Sox came on strong at the end behind the pitching of Steve Schneck, and some fine play by Valdez at short.

"A lot of times guys will fool you," notes Torchia. "A seventeenth-round draft pick could turn out to be a superstar. All they need sometimes is a chance to play. That's the beauty of this game. Valdez, for instance. He's shown so much progress, it's unbelievable. He hit .125 his first year and now he's tried switch-hitting and is up about .260. They call him 'Spider Man.' It's a lot of satisfaction to see their progress, really."

In the intimacy of the long season, emotional attachments are naturally developed with the players. This can become painful when the umbilical cord is cut.

"It's tough on us coaches that have developed these players to see them go," says the dark-haired Bristol manager. "Of course I feel better when I know they will help the big club."

And when they're traded to another organization?

"I wish all these kids well, except when they play us. I pick up the paper every day to see how they're doing."

One player whom Torchia followed particularly in 1978 was Ted Cox, who was traded to the Cleveland Indians in the deal for Dennis Eckersley. Cox made the appropriate stops up Boston's minor league ladder until making the top rung at Pawtucket as the International League's Most Valuable Player in 1977. "It's wonderful to see their progress," Torchia says. "They have ability when they first enter professional ball, but they don't know how to play the game. By the time they get to Triple-A, you can really see the difference. They amaze you. Cox hit only three or four homers here one year, then had fifteen or sixteen at Triple-A in three months before he got hurt."

That six-player trade, by the way, underscored Boston's position among the royalty of baseball organizations.

"I know that there's more people in the big leagues who came through the Boston farm system than any other team right now," says Torchia, making his assessment in late August of 1978. "Baltimore was ahead of us, but after we made that trade with Cleveland, that moved us over the Orioles."

The bulletlike cracks of batting practice serve as a background symphony for Torchia's dialogue. Now he is making a point about the well-heeled Boston farm system, that the reason it is so good is because of dedicated and loyal people like himself. ("I have been with the Red Sox for seventeen years, so my first love is the Red Sox.") It helps to be with an organization you like when conditions are sometimes as difficult as they are in the minors.

"There are very few scheduled days off, if any," says Torchia, emphasizing one of the biggest banes of minor league life. "I think we have something like one or two for the whole season. You're talking about playing 140 games in 4½ months. It's brutal."

Torchia changes his stance in the dugout, looking toward left field now where his players are shagging fly balls.

"You run into bad playing surfaces, bad lights, infields that have a lot of holes. Of course, that's good for the players in a way—if they can show well in those conditions, they can do well in the big leagues."

Torchia adds a final thought before joining his team on the field.

"The pay is not that good and the meal money's not that good. I tell my kids they're playing for a chance to make the majors—not to worry about making money here. They make just enough to get by."

He pauses to dramatize the point.

"They should accept that."

When Art Mazmanian was a struggling, skinny infielder in the New York Yankee chain back in the 1950s, he was expected to do things beyond his natural powers. "They wanted me to be a home run hitter," he says. "I never hit a home run in my life. They also tried to make a shortstop out of me, but my position was really second base." It might not have improved his ballplaying any at the time, but perhaps it made him a better manager in later life. It was a lesson in tolerance that he often translates to his players at Oneonta.

"I tell my players that I never expect them to make great plays—just make the routine play and make it every time," says the manager of the Oneonta Yankees. "That's what loses games, the inability to make the routine play. All I want is the Pony League play, the play that a fourteen year old can make."

Mazmanian's natural affinity for the young is evident, an inclination that is absolutely necessary at the Class A level of baseball where caring means as much as teaching. ("The way I treat my players is the same way I treat my kids. I'm not going to baby them. It's the kids who haven't been babied who survive.")

As strict as any parent would be, Mazmanian drums in lessons with tedious precision—even to the point of embarrassment. "Some managers frown on my methods, I know that," Mazmanian says. "But I'm not thinking of today. I'm thinking of the future. I would rather that the players' embarrassment take place here than in Yankee Stadium. If a kid misses first base, I'll make him go back and step on it—even if it is before 4,000 people. Sometimes, it rubs people the wrong way. But it's important that the players trust me that I'm doing it for their own good."

The word "trust" is an important part of Mazmanian's baseball vocabulary—a golden rule for him whether his work is on a professional level at Oneonta, N. Y., or back in California, where he is head baseball coach at Mt. San Antonio College. "A player should trust his coach," he says. "That's how I recruit at home. If you don't feel I'm fair and honest, you should not come to my school. I treat those students the same way I would treat the pros, so when they turn pro, it won't be a new experience for them. I don't think I'm easy to play for; I'm not primarily interested in being their friend. I'm interested in teaching baseball."

Few do it as well as Mazmanian, who has coached on both the high school and college level and managed professional teams for more than three decades. Before that, he had big league aspirations, like

any youngster coming out of high school. Rod De-
deaux, the well-known coach at the University of
Southern California, apparently saw promise in the
young infielder because he offered him a scholarship
when he graduated from Dorsey High in Los Angeles, which also produced the redoubtable Sparky Anderson. Mazmanian played on Southern Cal's first
national championship team, in the 1940s, then was
signed by the Yankees. His ascendancy in the organization took the natural steps, until an arm in-
jury and an inability to gain weight curtailed his career. His prospects for making the majors with the
Yankees were pretty bleak, anyway, with the
dynamic Phil Rizzuto and Billy Martin up ahead of
him. Thus he turned to managing in 1956, with the
Kansas City Athletics' rookie club in the Nebraska
State League. Subsequent stops took him to the Los
Angeles Dodger farm club at Twin Falls, Idaho, in
the Pioneer League; the San Francisco Giants' farm
team at Great Falls, Montana; and the Baltimore
Orioles' club in the Appalachian League in Virginia
before he took over the Oneonta Yankees in 1977.
Not incidentally, he led Oneonta to the New York-
Penn League pennant that year with a relatively
green team. And therein lies a favorite Mazmanian
story.

"We were a mediocre ballclub with a 7–7 record
and were coming back from a long, tiring road trip.
We got to bed about six o'clock in the morning, I
remember, and had to play a doubleheader that
same day. Well, we put on as miserable a performance as you could imagine. Not just that we made

errors; there was no hustle, no fire . . . there was nothing. So I waited until all the people left the ballpark, the lights were still on, and I took the kids down to the right field area and told them that I was absolutely embarrassed by their lack of effort. You played like you were tired, I told them, and now I'm going to give you a reason to be tired. And so I ran them, and ran them and ran them. And I said, every time you play that way, this is what we're going to do, so that at least I'll know why you're tired. And you know, from that day on, we became a different ballclub . . . won something like seventeen straight or seventeen of eighteen. The difference in a team sometimes is so small. In baseball, it's talent that wins, but that still doesn't excuse you from putting out the same effort, regardless of the talent. You don't have to have talent to put out the effort. That takes desire, and if you don't have that desire, you don't belong here; you don't belong in a Yankee uniform!"

Mazmanian has the look of a classic father figure —snow-white hair framing a cheery, tanned face and an aura of concern and sincerity when he speaks. His demeanor can be an obvious comfort to a young boy far from home chasing impossible dreams.

"The transition is very difficult to professional baseball," says Mazmanian, "so I make it a special point to emphasize togetherness . . . learning to like each other. Every team I've been with, I've emphasized this from day one. Players get off in cliques and Latins won't get along with whites, and whites with blacks, and so forth. You can battle for a job, but it has nothing to do with the way you treat each other. If the players are happier, it causes less homesickness."

Mazmanian is fully aware of the impressionable age of most Class A ballplayers and believes, as many do, that this level is the most important in their professional development. Thus, he takes his responsibilities seriously. "These kids are extremely receptive to teaching and coaching—more so than on any other level. So what's important from my standpoint is that judgments and decisions should be right and fair. The biggest mistake a coach makes is to allow his fondness for a certain type of individual weigh over a kid's talent. It costs you in sports . . . it's damaging to the kid. All of my players know what their weaknesses are—what they have to work on to get to the major leagues."

For most of them, the major leagues are a never-never land. Many are lucky just to move out of Class A ball to the next level.

"When this season is over," Mazmanian says, "probably just 20 percent of the guys from this league will still be playing in a year and a half. Of the thirty players from last year's championship team at Oneonta, only fifteen are still playing today. Next year, probably some of them will drop out."

Among the most important of the learning processes on the Class A level is the ability to recognize types of pitches. It is one of the basic things which distinguishes Single-A ball from Double-A, according to Mazmanian.

"These kids swing at pitches now that two to three years from now they won't swing at. In two to three years, they'll recognize a curve ball. Now they don't recognize it in time. A pitcher throws a curve that looks like a fastball, and the batter commits himself too early. They're more selective in Double-A."

Among the players whom Mazmanian has helped grow into big league manhood have been Jose Santiago, Jerry Remy, Butch Metzger, Doug Bird, Johnnie LeMaster, Pete Falcone, and Jack Clark. If it hadn't been for Mazmanian's intervention, Clark today may have been a struggling pitcher instead of a sensational outfielder for the San Francisco Giants.

"Clark wanted to be a pitcher," Mazmanian remembers of their association at Great Falls in the early 1970s. "He had a palm ball and a super arm. But he was too good a hitter to be a pitcher, and we made an outfielder out of him. He reminded me a little of Joe DiMaggio, except that he was too lazy at first to be a center fielder. But he was only seventeen then. Now he's hustling like he should have been before, and he has a chance to be a Hall of Famer."

Not all of Mazmanian's assessments are correct, of course. Human fraility demands certain errors in judgment as it did one year at Great Falls.

"I had an Indian kid who had a terrific arm, but was wild as heck. I never gave him much of a chance. I'd throw him into the game for an inning or two when it was out of hand. By August, he might have a total of seven innings compiled. Anyway, we were once making this long trip from Great Falls to

Ogden, Utah—about twelve or thirteen hours. And whenever we made trips like that, I would never use one of my good pitchers because the players would be so tired, they wouldn't give him much hitting support. So I told this Indian kid he was going to pitch the game in Ogden. Here it is, half the season is gone, and it's his first start. What I didn't know was that it was his eighteenth birthday and his family was coming down to see him pitch. Well, he throws a no-hitter for $6\frac{2}{3}$ innings and ends up pitching a beautiful game. Now he's up in the majors, pitching beautiful ball for the Oakland A's—John Johnson. That's the kid, and I didn't give him a chance to pitch for five weeks!"

Making Mazmanian's job even tougher these days is the present fast life-style of the minor leagues which allows managers little time to judge talent. It's also tougher on the players.

"Baseball has speeded up the process of going to the majors," Mazmanian says. "In my day, there were forty-nine minor leagues. Now there are only fifteen or sixteen. What that has done is speed up your evaluation of players. The time factor is important. If they don't produce in a few years, you have to move them out. Kids better be prepared to hold that job right away—to be able to produce that first year."

If the pressures are similar on a managerial level, Mazmanian does not seem to mind them. Along with his foremost job of teaching baseball, he is also a den mother, part-time psychologist, and father confessor for some twenty-odd players. In addition, he has the tedious duty of making daily reports to the parent team in New York on each game. ("You might get back home by four o'clock in the morning, but you still have to make that phone call.") Mazmanian is also asked by the Yankees to grade *every* player in the New York-Penn League twice— at the middle and end of the season.

"The reports are the part most managers dislike," Mazmanian says, "but I don't mind them. This job is so enjoyable that time goes by very fast for me."

Mazmanian's enthusiasm for the game is catching —which is why his teams usually win more than they lose, and Mazmanian continually wins respect.

"Baseball shouldn't be drudgery," he says. "It should be fun. There are ten teams in this league and for at least three of them, baseball seems like drudgery. That scares me. I don't ever want it to get that way. It's the *desire* to win that's so important, not winning itself. I can take a loss as well as anybody. The thing I could never stand was to go through the motions: just to sit there and let the other team beat you and not bust your neck to try to keep from losing."

Rooted on the lowest rung of the professional baseball ladder, Mazmanian expresses no special ambitions to move up. It seems that he has found the inner peace for which most men search a lifetime.

"I'm a Christian and the Lord leads my ways," he says. "I went to Southern Cal because He wanted me there. I'm here because He wants me here. If He wanted me in the big leagues, I would have made it.

If the Lord feels I belong here, this is where I'm going to be and I'll be perfectly content. I have a home life, my teaching. I have my cake and I'm eating it, too. I can't have it any more rewarding than when a kid says, 'Thank you,' when the year's over."

9

A Tale of Three Cities

The home of the El Paso Diablos of the Texas League is just a short pitch away from the Rio Grande among a jumble of decaying barrio projects. It is an antique among baseball parks, nearly six decades old with fading lights and rickety fences. The seating accommodations are extremely modest—wooden benches, folding chairs, or grass. The scoreboard is hand-operated and hardly a sight for sore eyes. And the center fielder has to run uphill to catch deep flies because the raised bank of a canal runs behind the outfield. It is not the best place in the world to either play or watch baseball.

But Diablo fans obviously don't come to Dudley Field to see an electronic scoreboard, sit in air-conditioned comfort, or dissect the finer points of the game. They come because they're part of the show—Jim Paul's show. Paul, owner, general manager, and sole administrative employee of the Diablos, has perfected the art of participatory baseball. One of the most popular of the Diablo rituals, for instance, is called "Bye, Bye, Baby." When fans arrive at the park, they are all handed a white Kleenex, which they wave vigorously while singing Janis Joplin's "Bye, Bye, Baby" whenever an opposing pitcher is driven from the game. A few pitchers will respond to this ceremony with an unkind gesture of their own (for which the Texas League has a standard fine, incidentally). In response to these Diablo theatrics, the archrival Midland Cubs have taken to waving towels from the dugout whenever an El Paso pitcher is knocked out of a game.

Along with the notorious "Bye, Bye, Baby" ritual, fans have been known to line up along the third base seats at Dudley Field and stuff dollar bills into the cap of a Diablo player whenever he hits a home run.

The inspiration point for all this well-planned madness is a man who ironically is not a died-in-the wool baseball fan. ("Unless you know a hell of a lot about baseball," says Paul, "it's boring.") Paul obviously knows more about filling stadiums, as his record-breaking performances at El Paso have proven. In 1977, the Diablos set an all-time attendance mark of 217,345—more than any other Double-AA team and more than nineteen of the twenty-four Triple-A teams in the country. His 1978 performance at the gate was impressive, too, although baseball purists would deride his means. But Paul accepts his title as bush league promoter as a sort of badge of honor.

"They call me bush," he says, "and meanwhile the major leagues are starving to death."

For every one of the Diablos' sixty-eight home

games, Paul has a gimmick. Some nights he gives away prizes at the gate: hats, bats, jackets, wristbands, helmets, water pistols, kazoos, and bottles of soap bubbles. "Yeah, it's great to see 5,000 people blowing bubbles in the stands," he says. "It's like Lawrence Welk." Paul once announced a Martinez Appreciation Night, and everyone with that last name was admitted free.

Once inside the park, Paul's self-styled "most unique show in baseball" begins. Public address announcer Mike Wall, a former disc jockey, gets out his kazoos, whistles, and toy horns and introduces each Diablo player in his red or canary-yellow uniform with the appropriate fanfare. The Diablos all feature official nicknames, such as: "The Eraser" Slater, "Honeybear" Rayford, "The Bobcat" Stupy, "Numbero Uno" Ramirez, and "The Masher" Clark. A visiting player steps out of a dugout branded "enemy" in enormous lowercase white letters, and as the batter walks to the plate, Wall gives away a bottle of champagne to the first twenty-five lucky number holders.

The rumble of the crowd increases and Paul's usual ebullience explodes to an even-higher pitch. "You gotta believe," he shouts while bustling around the stadium, then: "Nobody goes to sleep in *this* ballpark."

Wall now leads cheers over the overpowered PA system. He is a literal one-man band: he blows fanfares on his kazoo, claps rhythmically into the microphone, and exhorts the fans to chant, "Hit! Hit! Hit!" with such exuberance that the entire park shakes. When a hit follows there is a frenzy of screaming, hugging, and dancing in the aisles.

"There's nothing in baseball like it," says Paul, who bought the franchise in 1975 for $1,000 and a $50,000 debt. "The major leagues could learn a lot from us. Baseball is dying, and you can see why. I mean, look at who's running baseball today—a bunch of old farts smoking cigars. Just give me a shot at the major leagues. Give me a city like Houston for a year." Paul relishes the thought. "I mean no matter *what* I tried, it can't get any worse than it is now."

Buying a minor league baseball franchise these days, as anyone will tell you, is about as smart as investing in an hourglass factory. Caught in the shifting sands of time, the minors for the most part have diminished to a point of little return. So it was surprising in 1977 when the town of Visalia (pronouned Vye-SAIL-ya) California, went into the baseball business by including funds for a team in the Class A California League in its $14 million budget. As far as oldtimers at minor league headquarters could ascertain, it was the first municipally owned team in the history of organized baseball. Why did they go out on a limb like that? Civic pride, more than anything else.

"This is a good baseball town," says Pauline Taylor, coowner of a thriving hot dog stand at the corner of Center and Encina and one of the team's hottest supporters. "It's always been a good baseball town. We just had faith we could make it go."

It turned out that she and her neighbors were right. The team drew 44,747 spectators and cleared $621 in 1977. That was not enough of a profit to surpass walnuts, cotton, alfalfa, pomegranates, and barley as a mainstay of the local economy, but it sure beat losing money. And the team gave Visalia a deep source of pleasure and self-esteem. For twenty-seven of the past thirty-three seasons, Visalia has been a member of the storied California League, a circuit that dates back, in one incarnation or another, to the nineteenth century and has produced such alumni as Ping Bodie, Harry Hooper, Duffy Lewis, and more recently, Butch Wynegar, who played for the Reno Silver Sox in 1975 and jumped directly to the American League. Visalia's most distinguished alumnus was outfielder Vada Pinson, who went directly from eating Pauline Taylor's chili dogs to chewing steaks in Cincinnati.

Visalia's general success on the baseball field has been modest, the club's only pennants coming in 1971 and 1978, but there have been some singularly notable moments: Bud Heslet, who stayed on to become a Visalia fireman, hitting fifty-one home runs during the 1956 season; drawing 100,000 fans in 1947, which was ten times the population then.

The town had no team in 1976, the New York Mets having pulled out after eight seasons, and Visalians decided they would not let another idle season go by. A drive was started to land another franchise and city fathers finally signed a working agreement with the Minnesota Twins. The campaign's success was largely the result of the enthusiasm of Deputy City Manager Dick Anthony and Mrs. Taylor.

After the moderately successful 1977 season at the box office, 1978 was even better as the team showed well on the field with such fine talents as Steve Douglas, the California League's Most Valuable Player, league batting champion Joe Charboneau, and designated hitter Steve McManaman, one of the minors' top sluggers of 1978. These players made it a banner year as Visalia fashioned a 100–44 record, one of the best in all of baseball. The team drew 52,618 for sixty-five home games. It helped the team financially when Mrs. Taylor spearheaded pre-season ticket drives and the city did not compete against big league clubs in the scouting and signing of hot prospects. The Twins supplied most of the players and arranged the loan of the rest from other major league organizations. For instance, two players were on loan from the Los Angeles Dodgers and two from the Philadelphia Phillies in 1978.

Having players like Douglas and Charboneau, of course, had to hype the gate, but it wasn't the entire reason for Visalia's finish in the black during 1978.

"Attendance doesn't really tell the story," says Anthony. "It's how much you've got in the cashbox from box-seat sales, program advertising, ads on the outfield fence, and concession sales. You could put 100,000 people in our park and lose money; you could draw only 30,000 and make money. Ticket sales are less than half the revenue. Promoted right, an average team can make money; promoted wrong, a champion can lose. But promote right with a champion and you'll take money to the bank, baby."

The city already owned the little stadium where the team plays, Recreation Park, but while there is no rent to pay there are other costs such as maintenance of the field, players' equipment, hotel rooms, and road meals. The town of Visalia also foots the entire bill for bus transporation, umpires, the public address announcer, the official scorer, and the salary of general manager Jerry Lambert.

"Having the town own the team is quite an advantage," says Lambert. "We probably sell more season tickets and ads because of that, and a truck just dumped off ten bags of gympsun that were tacked on the end of the city order. Volume rates save a lot of money.

"It's a friendly little town. The thing that impressed me from the beginning is that everybody likes it here. Right after I arrived a guy told me, 'You know, this town's not on the major freeway, so people have to want to come here.' "

Not many outsiders do go to Visalia, a conservative place which offers little to sightseers other than a panoramic view of the lush San Joaquin Valley and James Earle Fraser's famous statue of a sagging Indian on his weary horse, *End of the Trail,* which stands in Mooney Grove Park. With a population edging past 40,000 now, Visalia is also proud of being not only the seat of Tulare County, but also the "Gateway to the Sequoias"—Sequoia National Park being about fifty miles to the east.

Baseball's return to the area in 1977 was a cause

for local celebration. The *Times-Delta* ("Oldest newspaper in the San Joaquin Valley") led the applause. "It's an understatement to say that people in this area missed the grand old game," the newspaper said and pointed out the obvious that the team would create jobs and increase revenues of many businesses in town.

One of the most timeless of baseball rituals, the choosing of a team nickname, was an important piece of business for Visalia. Teams there were formerly nicknamed Mets, Reds, Cubs, White Sox, A's, and Stars, but this time the general leaning was toward a sobriquet with more of a local flavor. Among those suggested were, "Minnows," "Pure Grits," "Doves," "Quails," and "Hot Dogs," the last perhaps as a tribute to the baseball-boosting Mrs. Taylor. But the final choice, a runaway one at that, was "Oaks," in deference to the fine oak trees which fill this clean, friendly city and which were once described in the diary of a wandering Spanish priest 172 years ago.

It seems that the team is now as firmly entrenched as those beloved oaks.

"One thing's for sure," says Mrs. Taylor. "Never again will the majors pack up and go home, leaving us without a franchise. It's ours now—here to stay as long as we want it."

Like millions of people, Ray Kuhlman loved baseball but was never good enough to play it professionally. So he did the next best thing—he bought his own team, the Kinston Eagles of the Carolina

League. Actually, he did more than buy the team, he put it together from scratch.

This do-it-yourself project germinated in February of 1978, when Kuhlman and his wife, Ruth, were scouting around for a team to invest in and "fell in love with Kinston" even though the last Carolina League entry died there in 1974 for lack of funds.

The Class A Carolina League "was a bit faster than I wanted to get into," said Kuhlman, but it didn't stop him from taking the plunge in the season of '78.

"I wanted to own a ballclub lock, stock, and barrel," he explains. "I knew there were plenty of players around who were released prematurely by major league organizations or who never had a chance."

The stewardship of the team was given to Leo Mazzone, a well-traveled veteran at thirty who had spent eleven years as a minor league pitcher and compiled an impressive record as a manager in the Class A Lone Star League. He was hired by Kuhlman in the dual capacity of manager and general manager. Mazzone brought in about a half-dozen players he knew from the Lone Star League and elsewhere, and Kuhlman promptly put them to work—selling season tickets, scoreboard advertising, and outfield billboards. By the week before opening day, Kuhlman had gathered eleven players of his own and had commitments from major league farm directors to supply eleven more.

He literally had a ballclub to call his own, since his was among only a handful of minor league teams in the country without a major league affiliation.

"What we're offering Kinston is a ballclub that's controlled here, not in some ivory tower," he proudly proclaimed.

But while glorying in his autonomy, Kuhlman was working at a distinct disadvantage. Kuhlman's costs were higher than most minor league teams, since he had to pay the salaries for the players not supplied on loan from the farm directors. The Eagles needed to take in about $150,000 in 1978, about twice what they would have to do with a major league affiliation.

That's why, for example, Kuhlman sometimes would ask umpires before games to "be gentle" about throwing baseballs out of play. Every ball thrown out or fouled into the stands cost Kuhlman $2. And when Kuhlman heard the sound of a bat breaking, he could also hear the sound of the cash register ringing. That would be another $5 gone.

To save on transportation, Kuhlman bought a used bus for road trips. It was driven by pitcher John Brownlee, who also picked up extra money doing the club's laundry. Brownlee and the other Eagles made an average salary of $500 a month.

Kuhlman did many things like that to save money, but it was the things he did not do that might have cost him more. Says a local newspaperman: "He didn't know how to promote the team very well. There were extremely few promotional nights at the ballpark, and that's the lifeblood of a minor league team."

Kuhlman also did not hire Jim Bouton when he

had a chance, losing a strong publicity factor.

"He is a very conservative baseball man," says one observer, "and Bouton, of course, has the image of being antiestablishment. Ironically, when Bouton went to the Savannah Braves, Terry Leach was knocked off their roster and signed with Kuhlman's team and became his ace relief pitcher."

Midway through the summer of 1978, it was apparent to Kuhlman that his team was going nowhere on the field or at the box office. "We leave more people on bases than Carter has peanuts," Kuhlman lamented while watching his pitching-rich, hitting-poor club finish last in the first half of the league's split season. The Eagles had plenty of strong pitching—typified by Tim Costello, who was dubbed "The Butcher" by some Kinston fans because of his shaved head. But they lacked players to drive in runs.

Even more distressing to Kuhlman was the fact that Kinston, population 22,000, did not share his passion for the team. The crowds averaged about 400 in Grainger Stadium, a place that seated 4,740.

"All I want to do is break even," Kuhlman said one summer night while watching his Eagles take a drubbing from the Alexandria Dukes and feeling himself take a bath at the gate as well.

It was apparent at this point that Kuhlman would not break even in his first year. In fact he would "lose his fanny," according to one reporter. Still, he was not about to jump off a light standard at Grainger Stadium.

"It's not accurate to say I don't give a damn about

money, but it's not my God," noted Kuhlman, a career airline pilot who has also served as a major league scout and organized a semipro team near his former home in Vienna, Va., a Washington suburb.

Near the end of the season, Kuhlman thoughtfully considered major league affiliation as a last-gasp measure to keep professional baseball in the small tobacco-growing community.

"The jury is still out on whether we're going to survive," Kuhlman said, "but I don't like the vibes I'm getting from the jury box. In hindsight, I think we might be asking too much of a town this size."

Some of his life savings lost, Kuhlman had however lost none of his heart at the end of a fallow season.

"People tell me I'm crazy," he said, "but it's what I want to do. I'd like to be here in fifteen years, still running the Eagles. But wherever I live, it's got to have baseball."

10

Never Standing Pat

"When he was out of baseball, Bill Veeck one time called me the most innovative guy in the game," Pat McKernan says.

That's a setup for one of McKernan's punch lines, a visitor soon finds out.

"Of course that sonofagun didn't hire me when he got back in."

McKernan's eyes twinkle as he pulls on a long drink of soda. He chuckles softly. The picture is of a man laughing at himself. And, in fact, that is one of McKernan's most appealing qualities: the lack of a stuffed-shirt image.

McKernan is a blue-collar worker in the business-suit world of the minor league hierarchy. Once owner of the Eastern League's Pittsfield Rangers, McKernan now is league president with few changes in the transition other than perhaps some more weight on his chunky frame.

He was once a svelte 189½ pounds, he remembers.

"But only for a minute and a half," says McKernan, whose famous hot dog diet at Pittsfield some years back was the talk of the minors.

In one of his more ingenious promotional schemes, McKernan announed that he would go on a protein diet, consuming merely hot dogs, until he brought his weight of 350 pounds down to a respectable figure. He would eat one hot dog for every 500 people that came to the ballpark.

"It was a big production-type thing," McKernan recalls. "You know, ceremony at home plate and the whole bit."

It took awhile, but the gimmick eventually raised attendance and lowered McKernan's weight.

"To show you what kind of a promotional genius I was, if that had been for the first ten days of my diet, I don't think I would have made it," McKernan says. "I don't think we drew 500 people to the park any of those first ten days!"

Attendance picked up also as McKernan passed out sunglasses one night.

"I did that when we put new lights in the park," he says with a grin, "you know, so the fans wouldn't become blind."

A player by the name of Jim Bottoms was made into a local legend by McKernan's promotional touch. Bottoms was married in a home plate ceremony—complete with crossed bats and rice. It was a terrific piece of business, except that not as many people saw it as McKernan would have wished.

"As it turned out," he says, "we had a carnival in our parking lot the same time. And for various reasons, you couldn't park cars there. The marriage ceremony didn't draw too well."

But it did stir interest. Soon, network television was showing its face in Pittsfield—to show McKernan's face to the nation. He remembers: "CBS was up here to do a feature on me, supposedly on how I was operating in the face of adversity. Which wasn't as adverse as people were writing about, but which always sounds great for publicity purposes. I went along with it. After all, I wasn't going to say, 'Sorry, sir, we're not as bad as you think.'"

Though McKernan downplays the situation in Pittsfield, it was bad enough for onetime owner Joe Buzas to give up the ship in 1969 and move the Boston Red Sox farm team out of town. McKernan, a onetime newspaperman in Batavia, N. Y., and general manager of a New York-Penn League team there for one year, signed on as the GM at Pittsfield under Buzas in 1965. He stayed in that capacity for five erratic seasons before Buzas was forced to close down operations.

"Actually, I recommended that he pull out," McKernan says. "And it sounds funny, because I later bought the franchise. But I told Joe it was no longer possible to make a return on his investment and still pay both our salaries. He knew that he had to go and I agreed with him. After he left, and I bought the franchise, it looked for a moment like I had given him false information. But now it was only paying one person, instead of two or three. That's why it could survive with one person owning it."

McKernan paid the unprincely sum of $1,000 for the franchise and soon had a working agreement with the Texas Rangers. Four years later, he would sell the team for $45,000, a 4,500 percent profit!

"It was sold so cheaply because that was the minimum you could buy a team for, and it had been turned into the league," McKernan explains. "It was sort of inside; few people knew it was available. There was one other person who had the option, but he wasn't interested in buying the team. Everyone knew me, so they voted it to me and I paid the minimum for it."

As ensuing years would show, McKernan was not only a promotional man, but a liberal man as well. He gave tryouts to players that other teams wouldn't touch—a female hotshot and the antiestablishment thinker, Jim Bouton. Both failed, but neither could say that McKernan didn't give each a chance.

"Jackie Jackson was the girl," McKernan says. "I didn't tell anyone she was coming up, but she leaked the story to one of the papers in Washington, and I took advantage of it. We had CBS up here again to do another feature on us."

Miss Jackson, a first baseman (or first basewoman, as the case may be), was a talented ladies softball player who was dying to show the world that she could swing as well with the men.

"People got nervous with the girl," says

McKernan, "asking if I was turning baseball into a circus. And I said, no, if she's good enough, there's no reason why she can't be signed. And there's no way you can stop it. I tell you the truth, I have never done anything in my promotions that would ridicule baseball, or do anything bad for it. I had a closed tryout for the girl; even though the media got in, I didn't let the fans in to watch. If she was good enough, I would have signed her. There might have been a whole lot of howling. But if you do things that are right, you can't get into trouble. Jackie could field pretty well, but she didn't hit. She was really a softball player who thought she was better than she was."

McKernan juggles the ice in his glass and laughs.

"Strange as it may seem, the more I thought of it, the more I wondered if *she* was really a *he*. Not that she looked masculine, or anything like that. She was very feminine-looking. But sometimes, somebody can dress up and fake you out . . . so I sent my wife, Anne, into the locker room with her to make sure. She was a girl, all right."

McKernan also knew that he would be swimming upstream in the Bouton case as well. The onetime star pitcher for the New York Yankees was not the most popular man in baseball after his *Ball Four* book had exposed the sport's soft underbelly. He had been making good money in television when he decided to chuck it all and try a comeback in baseball. Of course he went to McKernan for a tryout.

"Bouton was here about five days, working out

on the sidelines." remembers McKernan, "and I really wanted to sign him. But he wasn't good enough. See, he thinks I didn't sign him because I was pressured by baseball people. But I felt that if I signed him, it wouldn't have been fair to Bouton to let him be embarrassed just so I could make some money."

McKernan said he had "felt some pressure" from parts of baseball society, "but it wasn't to the degree that it would have stopped me" from signing Bouton. "He was supposedly going to work himself into shape and come back again. He had to go away for awhile, because at the time he was making some political speaking appearances. He said he would rejoin us on the road, I remember, in Elmira, N. Y., and he was supposed to travel with us and pitch with us for a week. And if he got into shape, I would look at him again. But he went home and decided not to, I guess."

Along with Bouton, an array of otherwise famous names has graced Pittsfield under McKernan's aegis —George Scott, Toby Harrah, Reggie Smith, Billy Madlock, Larry Biittner, and Dock Ellis. One year, Scott won the Triple Crown and the Eastern League pennant for Pittsfield all in one home run swing at his last time at bat. That same year, 1965, Billy McCloud had an 18–0 record for the Red Sox farm team.

"That helped ruin this town in the beginning," McKernan notes, "because teams after that could never come up to the standards of the 1965 club. We drew 79,000 here that year, but attendance slipped thereafter."

There was never a dull moment, though, with McKernan pulling his zany promotional stunts and an occasional riot to spice things up.

"One of the greatest fights of all time happened here," says McKernan, almost with a note of pride in his voice. "The night before in Waterbury, there was this collision at third base with our big first baseman, Al Thompson, sliding into this midget third baseman of theirs and breaking his leg. So the next night Waterbury was at our place and we were winning something like 12–2 and along about the seventh inning, they threw at Madlock. He went out after the pitcher with the bat and the catcher went after Madlock with his helmet. A guy comes out of the bullpen with a mask and starts swinging it, and everyone starts running around. We soon had the cops here and the ballplayers started fighting with them, too. They finally arrested one of the visiting ballplayers and we had to get him out of jail the next day and go to court."

McKernan continued to witness battles when he later assumed the league presidency, only now they were on a more subtle scale. They were taking place among the club owners.

"I guess the best way to describe my job is that I try to keep the owners from killing each other," McKernan says, chuckling. "It's a lot easier running a team than running a league, believe me. You're your own boss when you own a team. But in a league, everybody pulls in different directions, looking for his own benefit, and you have to worry that one doesn't benefit too much at the expense of another. You try to satisfy everybody, but every decision you make, somebody's going to be mad at you."

McKernan pauses for a drink of soda.

"You see, one of the main problems of a league president is that you have to solve everybody's problems and most of the time you're not there when something happens. Usually in the big leagues, you can see the videotape of an incident and make a decision from there. But here, you've got to go by an umpire's report. And if it's like the case of a player hitting an umpire, you almost have to take the ump's word for it. Usually you check with another person, whether it be the peanut vendor, or the groundskeeper, or somebody who agrees with the umpire. I get blamed for going with my umpires too much. But it's like the judge going with the police. You assume that if they bring a guy in, they must have a reason for it."

McKernan had one open-and-shut case, though, when one recent Eastern League game was disrupted by a comic argument over lighting.

"They were playing a game in a city which shall remain nameless," McKernan says, "when all of a sudden the lights go out. The umpire goes down to the groundskeeper and says, 'What happened?' The groundskeeper says, 'The park commissioner made me turn them off. He says we're wasting electricity.' This happens during a game! Finally, the park commissioner calls the cops and wants to have the umpire arrested for talking back to him. The riot squad comes in wondering what the hell is going on. Can you imagine? Anyway, it got settled. The lights went on. But that's what happens in the minor leagues ... that's what it's all about."

Though McKernan's impact on the minor leagues has been duly noted by the redoubtable baseball showman, Bill Veeck, among others, Pittsfield's free-thinker denies any association with greatness.

"I think part of my legend is that I always got along with writers so that they, in all honesty, built things up better than they actually were," McKernan tells you. "My promotions were good— but not all *that* good! You know, a guy becomes a famous ballplayer—maybe he's hitting well, but somebody makes his hits sound better. It's that type of thing."

McKernan is more apt to salute other people, like Veeck or Charlie Finley, for instance.

"Both of them should be in the Hall of Fame," McKernan says. "And when you say that about Charlie Finley, that's almost heresy. Most baseball people now would look at you with a jaundiced eye. But look at what he's done—he's got night World Series games, for instance. When he went to the colorful uniforms in Oakland, everyone thought he was crazy. But now everyone's wearing double-knits."

Despite hollering from baseball's hidebound conservatives, men with such theatrical flairs have obviously delivered new sock to the game and McKernan is wholly supportive of them.

"I think baseball is taking on more of a show business quality," notes McKernan. "You have to give fans more than just a baseball game. It's like a night out at the theater now. And they're showing the fruits—more crowds, more teams. Attendance is up in the minors, too."

And just where does McKernan see the minors going these days?

"We're certainly not dying," he says. "We're not young and eighteen anymore. But we are middle-aged and growing toward maturity—with some hopes."

Spoken like a true promotions man.

About the Author

Ken Rappoport is a veteran sportswriter with the Associated Press and has nine books to his credit, including the Tempo title *Great College Football Rivalries*. In addition, he has contributed to four other books and several national magazines. He resides in New Jersey with his wife Bernice and three children, Felicia, Sharon, and Larry. He has just completed a comprehensive history of the NCAA Basketball Championships entitled *The Classic*.